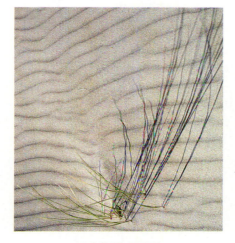

NUMBER THREE

Oregon Backroads

BY MARK HOY

AMERICAN GEOGRAPHIC PUBLISHING
HELENA, MONTANA

WILLIAM A. CORDINGLEY, CHAIRMAN
RICK GRAETZ, PUBLISHER
MARK THOMPSON, DIRECTOR OF PUBLICATIONS
BARBARA FIFER, ASSISTANT BOOK EDITOR

This series provides in-depth information about Oregon's geographical, historical, cultural and natural history subjects.
Design by Len Visual Design; Linda Collins, graphic artist. Printed in Hong Kong by Nordica International Ltd.

To Mom and Dad—who taught me
about the best things.

Library of Congress Cataloging-in-Publication Data
Hoy, Mark.
  Oregon backroads / by Mark Hoy.
    p.   cm. – (Oregon geographic series; no. 3)
  Bibliography: p.
  ISBN 0-938314-48-3 (pbk.): $14.95
  1. Oregon—Description and travel—1981—Tours   2.
Automobiles—Road guides—Oregon.   I. Title   II. Series.
F874.3.H68   1988
917.95′O443—dc 19   88-14569
                                                              CIP.

ISBN 0-938314-48-3
text © 1988 Mark Hoy
© 1988 American Geographic Publishing
Box 5630, Helena, MT 59604
(406) 443-2842

CONTENTS

Title page: *Sand Dunes National Recreation Area.* CHARLIE BORLAND
Facing page, left: *Along Little Sheep Creek in Wallowa County.*
STEVE TERRILL
Right: *Wildflowers bloom in profusion in a meadow near Mt. Hood.*
CHARLIE BORLAND
This page, top: *The mountain ranges and canyon country of southeastern Oregon are part of a landscape filled with surprises.*
DIANE KELSAY
Left: *A fisherman finds solitude on a rocky section of Oregon shoreline near Cannon Beach.* ANDREW E. CIER

Front cover, left: *Yaquina Bay oyster beds, Newport.* ANDREW E. CIER
Right: *Looking toward the Strawberry Mountains near Prairie City.*
STEVE TERRILL

Introduction

WHEN A GUIDE IS NOT A GUIDEBOOK

Above: *Poppies color the spring landscape in the Wallowa Mountains in northeastern Oregon.* **Right:** *A dense thicket guards the life-giving waters of Somer's Creek in Hells Canyon National Recreation Area.* DAVID JENSEN PHOTOS

The people and places described in this book are the highlights of 15 years of travel around the state of Oregon. They are part of an on-going exploration that's become so much a part of my life that it roughly qualifies as the answer to the question "What do you do for a living, anyway?"

Often, I'm searching for material for magazine articles, most frequently for *Northwest* magazine, the Sunday supplement to the state's largest newspaper, the Portland *Oregonian*. But almost as often, I've had other reasons for exploring the Oregon Country. Sometimes it's a road trip in search of the perfect trout stream, or perhaps a simple escape from city tensions. There's something about a campsite overlooking a stretch of Pacific Ocean beach, or a frosty alpine lake in the Cascades, or a desert hot spring in Eastern Oregon that seems to help keep things in perspective. In fact, looking back on those 15 years, I realize I've found some of my best places when I wasn't really looking for anything at all.

Which is why this book is a guide, but not a guide-book. You won't find information here on every motel, highway rest stop and roadside cafe in Oregon. That's been done, accurately and well, by other writers and by the professionals at the state tourism office—and I've listed what I think are the most helpful of those guidebooks in the reference sections for each chapter. This book is something different. It's meant to be selective and highly personal. If I've described a resort or an activity, it means I've been there and enjoyed myself—probably because of the hosts or people who made my experience memorable in some way. Or maybe it's because there weren't many (or any) other people there and I enjoyed the quiet and solitude. Either way, I hope you can get a feeling for the genuinely warm people and the unmatched scenic variety of Oregon.

I'd like it if this book pointed you in some intriguing directions. I know I've probably missed as much as I've covered but there's an element in that omission that's exciting, for me at least. Maybe the best sights and the most interesting people are still out there, awaiting discovery.

Which brings me around to getting there. Some of my friends enjoy bad-mouthing travel on the interstate highways. All right, they say, you drive through some fantastic country on the interstate, but at 65 miles an hour, it's like watching a movie (complete with your own soundtrack, in many cases)—and with the same low level of personal involvement. I guess I can't be quite that harsh, because by necessity I do quite a bit of traveling that way every year. If you need to get from one place to the next, the interstate highway system saves hours of driving time—and you do see some beautiful scenery.

But seeing the country and experiencing it are two different things. You really can't expect to appreciate the countryside—and especially the people who live there—until you slow down. Get yourself a good road map of Oregon, so you won't get lost (when you don't want to!). Make it a point to get out of your car and talk to people along the way. Believe it or not, most people in Oregon still talk to strangers. Even today, with so many journalists and TV personalities describing every conceivable travel destination—over and over again, it seems—the Oregon Country still holds some secrets. In its variety of mountains, deserts, beaches and rushing rivers, there's still a chance for discovery, an opportunity to challenge yourself. And along the way, there's a good chance you'll meet others who are looking for the same challenges, and finding out some things about themselves. Perhaps we'll meet one day, out there on one of those less-traveled paths.

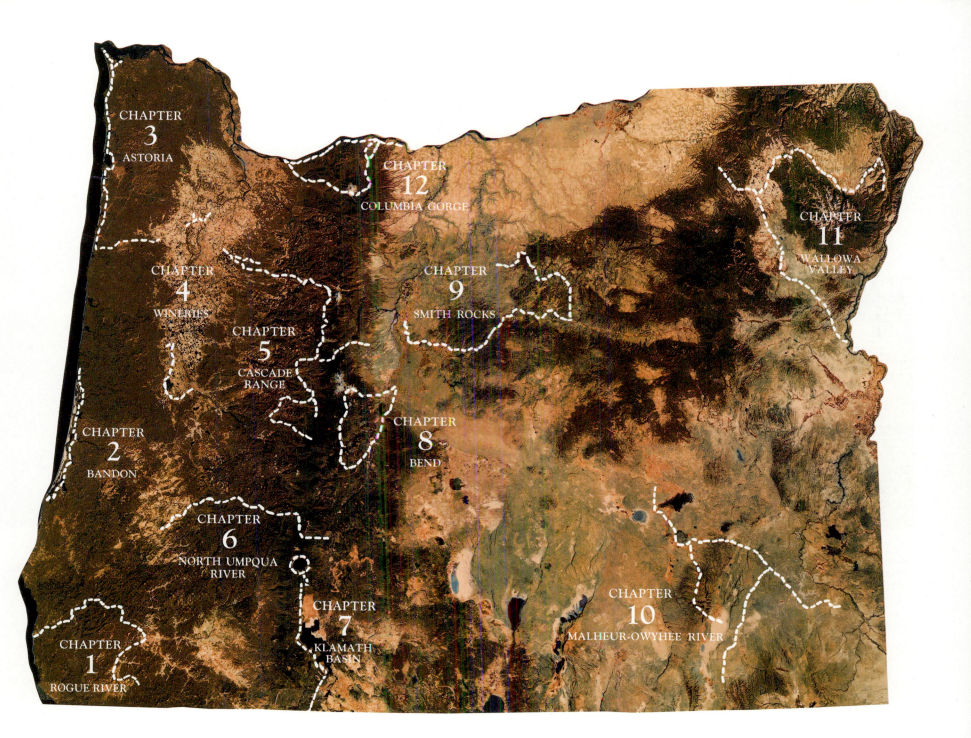

CHAPTER
3
ASTORIA

CHAPTER
12
COLUMBIA GORGE

CHAPTER
11
WALLOWA
VALLEY

CHAPTER
4
WINERIES

CHAPTER
9
SMITH ROCKS

CHAPTER
5
CASCADE
RANGE

CHAPTER
8
BEND

CHAPTER
2
BANDON

CHAPTER
6
NORTH UMPQUA
RIVER

CHAPTER
10
MALHEUR-OWYHEE RIVER

CHAPTER
7
KLAMATH
BASIN

CHAPTER
1
ROGUE RIVER

Rogue River & Southwestern Oregon

OREGON CAVES NATIONAL MONUMENT
ROGUE RIVER
ILLINOIS RIVER
HALF MOON BAR LODGE
KALMIOPSIS WILDERNESS

Above: *A wild iris in bloom in the Rogue River canyon.* ANCIL NANCE
Right: *A Rogue River drift boat and passengers float safely through "The Horn" in tumultuous Blossom Bar rapids.* DIANE KELSAY

On my first visit to Oregon—more years ago than I care to admit—I drove the scenic highway along the south coast, after a damp camping trip in the redwoods of northern California. The strongest memories from my first hour in Oregon revolve around the stark beauty of that coastline drive and my first passage over the Rogue River bridge at the little town of Gold Beach. I remember wondering why the Rogue River was so famous. After all, from my vantage point on U.S. Highway 101, the Rogue looked like any other coastal river. It just wound down through a flat tidal plain from the east and dumped directly into the ocean, with almost no estuary or bay to mark its end. Now I've learned that you can't begin to know a scenic treasure like the Rogue River from the driver's seat of your car. And I wish I'd taken a right turn—on that first trip—and explored the road that parallels the river upstream.

Most visitors get their first look at the Rogue River farther inland, as they zip along Interstate 5 between Medford and Grants Pass. That's a nice stretch of river—there aren't any ugly sections of the Rogue—but when the freeway turns north past Grants Pass, the river heads west toward the Pacific Ocean. And that's where the true character of the Rogue River really begins to surface.

It's the hundred-mile stretch of the Rogue that Congress focused on when it designated the Rogue River as one of the original seven Wild and Scenic Rivers in 1968. For a sample, take the Merlin exit off Interstate 5 just north of Grants Pass and make the scenic, 20-minute drive to the Grave Creek bridge. There you'll discover the beginnings of the Rogue River canyon. For the next 40 miles downstream, there is no road access at all to the Rogue. The canyon, however, is not the river's beginning; the Rogue emerges from the Western Cascades, far to the east.

The Rogue River runs through a steep, heavily forested canyon that in many ways is a time capsule, preserving centuries of lore and legend. The original human residents, the Rogue Indians, prospered on the bountiful fish runs, wild game and other food resources of the canyon. The Rogues had a reputation among coastal tribes as fierce warriors, and the U.S. Army was hard-pressed to dislodge them from their homeland in a series of skirmishes, called the Rogue Indian Wars, from 1855 to 1856. Several battles in this frontier war are commemorated at campsites along the river, including one site where the Rogue Indians managed to rout the troops by rolling boulders down on the soldiers' camp from a bluff above the river.

After the native bands were scattered, gold miners flocked to the canyon, lured by the yellow nuggets that still occasionally can be plucked from a sand bar along the Rogue. Seams of gold, located farther up the canyon walls, were mined with huge, high-pressure nozzles and the ore crushed by giant stamp mills, which had to be packed into the canyon—piece by piece—on the backs of mules. Some of these hulks still can be seen, rusting quietly along the river. Chinese gold miners also played an early role in settling the Rogue canyon, but most of their new-found riches were shipped back to the mother country and they left behind only place names, such as China Gulch.

Although some dreamers still pan for gold in the Rogue's sandy washes, most visitors today are lured by other precious commodities—the river's thrilling white water and the big salmon and steelhead that fight their way up from the ocean through the Rogue's rapids to its mountain tributaries. The roadless stretch below Grave

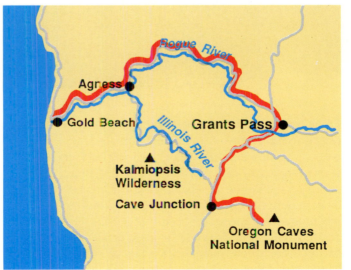

Above: *Whitewater rafting on the Rogue River continues to grow in popularity, despite a limited-entry permit system.* ANCIL NANCE

Two paddlers navigate their inflatable kayak, sometimes called an orange torpedo, through the fish ladder at Rainie Falls.
LYSBETH CORSI PHOTO, TOM STACK & ASSOCIATES

Facing page: *Hikers along the Rogue River trail enjoy a unique perspective.* DIANE KELSAY

Creek becomes a white-water enthusiast's dream, dropping through a series of spine-tingling rapids separated by quiet, even-flowing pools, ideal for lying back and gazing at the spectacular canyon scenery that slides past. Most rapids on the Rogue are challenging, but can be negotiated by experienced boaters. The exception is Rainie Falls, where the river encounters a stub of erosion-resistant lava and the entire flow drops 12', straight down. All boats, except those whose pilots harbor a death wish, must be hand-lined down a fish ladder next to the falls.

Early settlers in the Rogue Valley believed that anyone who tried to run the rapids from Grants Pass down through the canyon to the ocean was courting certain death. Pioneer boatman Glen Wooldridge and his friend Cal Allen proved them wrong by piloting a wooden boat they'd built themselves all the way through the canyon to Gold Beach in 1915. They were forced to portage around several bad rapids, including Blossom Bar, which still is considered the most difficult white-water stretch on the Rogue. Wooldridge later succeeded in dynamiting a clear channel, used today, through the rocks at Blossom Bar.

In 1925, writer Zane Grey, hired a local guide named Claude Barton to take him, his fishing party, and their wooden boats down through the Rogue canyon. Grey's party probably was the first to run the river for pure sport—they'd come to enjoy the fabulous fishing for summer steelhead (ocean-going rainbow trout). But his written account makes it clear that he got more excitement than he bargained for: one of their boats was completely destroyed in the rapids and most of the others sustained heavy damage during the rocky passage. Today's sophisticated inflatable rafts and aluminum drift boats make the trip down the Rogue seem almost tame by comparison. Still, experienced boatmen say you never can take this river for granted. The best way to run the Rogue—or any wild river—for the first time is with a guide. Outfitters provide the right type of boats or rafts and have years of experience at running rapids. In addition, they provide camping gear, serve up plenty of hearty food in camp, and even supply fishing gear if you need it.

Inflatable kayaks, sometimes called orange torpedoes, also have become popular in the Rogue canyon in recent years. They resemble miniature canoes, are piloted by just one person, and allow for more freedom, maneuverability and thrills than a raft. My float trip a few years ago through the Wild Section of the Rogue in an inflatable kayak was an experience I'll never forget.

Our guides split the party into groups of four or five kayaks each. After learning the basics of control in our little craft, we plunged immediately into the rapids at Grave Creek, Tyee, Wildcat, Black Bar and Horseshoe Bend. Everyone in the group was unceremoniously dumped out of a kayak at least once in the middle of a frothing rapid, but the water was warm, we all wore life jackets, and our guides kept us out of danger. On the third day of the trip, before we entered the narrow canyon called Mule Creek and shot through the big white water below at Blossom Bar, we were one nervous group. None of us could even look at breakfast! But with a strong rush of adrenaline and shouts of encouragement from our guides, we ran the rapids in fine style. In the past two decades, the Rogue River has gained national fame as a Wild & Scenic River. Each year, more boaters and anglers flock to the canyon. On some summer weekends, the number of people who come to experience the Rogue's delights threatens to destroy the very thing they are out to enjoy.

That's why a strict permit system was set up several years ago to regulate the number of rafting or fishing trips on the Rogue River. Permits are divided between private parties and outfitters' groups, which means that the easiest way to ensure a float down the Rogue is to sign up for a guided trip. Private parties must enter a lottery for permits held each spring. But every year some permits go unused, so it's almost always possible to float the river—if you understand the system. Write the Rand Visitor Center for more information on permits.

Running the Rogue River in a white-water craft is exciting, but there are many other ways to get to know the Rogue canyon. Hiking all, or part, of the 40-mile trail that parallels the river on its north bank gives you a completely different perspective, even if you've boated the river many times. The trail is level and well maintained, with a few switchback grades up and down the side canyons, where tributary streams enter the main river. A hiker can take time to stop and look, explore the tributary canyons, or slowly fish downstream through some particularly enticing stretch of river.

Many hikers carry all their gear in backpacks and stop each night at designated campsites along the river. Others take advantage of the lodges, located at intervals along the river. The Rogue lodges were established to cater to fisherman, but now are happy to offer their services to rafters and hikers as well—if you can plan your trip in advance and make reservations.

There are seven river lodges scattered through the Wild River section of the Rogue canyon. Several other

lodges cluster along the river outside the Wild River section and are accessible by road. Most of the Wild River lodges are small, originally set up to serve the 12 to 18 fishermen and guides on a typical float trip. The canyon lodges also must bring in all their supplies by boat, since they have no road access. They plan their meals carefully, relying on reservations made in advance. That's why they can't accommodate "drop-in" guests off the trail or river.

The canyon lodges are comfortably rustic, offering the luxury of beds and clean sheets, and they serve copious amounts of home-style food. Most cater to guests only from May until November, and the people who operate them are a breed apart.

Willis Krause and his wife run the lodge at Half Moon Bar, a short distance downstream from the Blossom Bar rapids. Willis is a quiet, serious type of person who enjoys the solitude of life in the Rogue canyon. He's built along the lines of a slim rock climber and he guided professionally before he settled at Half Moon Bar. Now he scrambles up the jagged slopes of the Rogue canyon in search of his own brand of inner peace. Along the way he's found several old "vision quest" sites, places where the Rogue Indians searched for their personal spirit guides.

Across the river, Allen Boice manages Paradise Lodge in a totally different style. A large, gregarious man, Allen can usually be found on the long deck outside the lodge's dining room, overlooking the river, puffing on his pipe and greeting guests as they arrive. Allen is a former sheriff from Curry County, through which the Rogue runs. During his term of office he was often controversial, with outspoken opinions. But to see him now, surveying the river and chatting comfortably with one and all, you'd have to believe he's left all that controversy and stress behind, somewhere downriver.

The jet boats that deliver passengers to Half Moon Bar and Paradise Lodge, as well as to all the other lodges on the lower river, are a story all their own. Glen Wooldridge, in addition to his historic first downstream passage on the Rogue, also is credited with running the first power boat all the way upstream through the canyon from Gold Beach to Grants Pass. He did it in 1947 with a 22-horsepower outboard motor. Others soon learned the trick and motorboats eventually took over from the mule trains that had delivered the mail upriver to the lodges and other homesteaders.

One of the three companies that now operate commercial jet boats on the lower Rogue still has a contract to deliver the mail, but one look at their boats tells you that they are primarily in the passenger business. The sleek jet boats carry 30 to 60 passengers and move rapidly upstream by shooting a powerful jet of water out the back—with no propellers to hang up on rocks, so they can operate in as little as six inches of water. Today, these 1,000-horsepower jets run all the way from Gold Beach upriver to Blossom Bar, a round trip of more than 100 miles, and offer a thrilling run through the rapids, comparable to any amusement park ride.

The jet boats are also a boon to hikers who would rather not hike the whole 40 miles of the Rogue River trail.

If you make your arrangements in advance, the jet boats can function like big taxis, dropping you and your gear off at a convenient stop along the river, then picking you up later at another pre-arranged spot.

Combine this taxi service with the overnight accommodations at the lodges and you have a world of possibilities for anyone with an itch to explore the lower Rogue canyon. If you don't plan on camping, have the jet boat drop you and your gear off at a lodge. After a big breakfast next morning, hike downstream on the trail to another lodge. Later, you might arrange to be picked up downstream by a jet boat—or hike to the trailhead where you parked your car. It's simple if you just plan ahead! Spring is definitely the prime time for hiking the Rogue River trail. The wildflowers in the canyon put on a show and the lodges aren't booked up with rafters or anglers until later in the season. Summer is the most popular season for a rafting trip, since the water and weather will have warmed up enough to make for great swimming and sunbathing. In the fall, fishermen descend on the Rogue River in force, greeting the runs of returning salmon and steelhead in September with an array of baits, lures and bright flies.

But if you really value your solitude and quiet, try a winter visit to the lower Rogue. It seldom snows in this part of Oregon—weather forecasters refer to it as the state's "banana belt"—and the winter steelhead fishing can be surprisingly productive.

The Rogue River and its surrounding area offer such a diverse choice of outdoor activities, there's been talk recently of a new national park in the area. Supporters are calling it the Siskiyou National Park and, as now proposed, it would include much of the Rogue River canyon and the area around it currently protected as wilderness, as well as some other areas nearby.

The Illinois River, one of the Rogue's largest tributaries, joins the main river at the little town of Agness. Well known for excellent fishing in the first four or five miles above its junction with the Rogue, the Illinois also challenges expert boaters with its white-water rafting. Its confined canyon requires quick maneuvering in heavy rapids. But rafting on the Illinois is possible only during the spring run-off season. After the spring rains end, the river usually drops to a level that features more rocks than water in the riverbed. A fine hiking trail also parallels part of the Illinois River. It traverses country where you're less likely to find human company than on the Rogue River trail, but there are trade-offs. The area is rugged, traversing many steep canyons carved by the river and its tributary streams over the millennia. Hiking here requires both strength and stamina.

The Illinois River hiking trail leads into the Kalmiopsis Wilderness, one of the least-visited wilderness areas in Oregon. The Kalmiopsis area, and its Babyfoot Lake, and nearby Eightdollar Mountain, is home to several species of very rare plants, some of which are found nowhere else in the world. The soil here, which was originally part of the ocean floor, contains such high concentrations of magnesium and other metals that plants have been forced to adapt to an environment that would normally be considered toxic.

Nearby is the state's only underground park, Oregon Caves National Monument. Follow U.S. Highway 199—which connects Crescent City, California, and Grants Pass, Oregon—to the little town of Cave Junction. Take State Highway 46 east for 20 miles until it dead-ends high in the Siskiyou Mountains at the monument grounds. This access road is a twisting, narrow affair that's a travel experience all its own—definitely not recommended for cars towing trailers or for anything but four-wheel-drive vehicles in the winter when it's icy.

Once you've arrived, a guide will lead you on a 75-minute walking tour down into Oregon Caves. It's actually one long cave, with many connected passages and rooms, eroded from a beautiful marble formation. Colorful formations of calcite—in the form of stalactites (reaching down from the ceiling), stalagmites (reaching up from the floor), and columns (where the two meet)—grace the chilly interior of the cave. The tour allows visitors a glimpse of the powerful geological forces that shaped both the surrounding Siskiyou Mountains and the caverns themselves.

Outside, several nature trails above the cave offer outstanding views of the surrounding mountains. In summer, the Oregon Caves Chateau, a six-story, rustic lodge, offers comfortable accommodations. Don't miss its

grand dining room, with fine linen tablecloths, big picture windows and a trout stream that runs right through the building!

On the return trip from Oregon Caves, consider a stop at Siskiyou Vineyards, on Oregon Highway 46 just six miles east of Cave Junction. This winery produces fine wines that exhibit some intriguing characteristics—they're a cross between the popular California wines produced from grapes grown in the sunny climate farther south and the distinctive new Oregon wines taking hold in the Willamette Valley to the north.

Eightdollar Mountain and the nearby Kalmiopsis Wilderness are home to several species of plants found nowhere else in the world
DIANE KELSAY

Facing page: *The Siskiyou Mountains are traversed by the Illinois River in an area that has been promoted as a new national park.*
GEORGE WUERTHNER

Bandon Land

Above: *Shifting sand dunes along the Oregon coast.*
DIANE KELSAY
Right: *A surf-carved rockscape near Cape Arago.* CHARLIE BORLAND

Oregon's south coast is a place of rugged beauty, with sweeping ocean vistas and pastoral river valleys winding down to sandy beaches. Life proceeds here at a little slower pace, in rhythm with the tides and seasons. The people in the little towns strung along U.S. Highway 101, like coastal village dwellers around the world, have learned to be independent, persevering and patient. And along Oregon's south coast, they've learned to love their quiet corner of the world intensely.

My favorite town on the south coast is Bandon. Like many of its neighbors along Highway 101, Bandon was sited on the estuary of a major coastal river, in this case the Coquille River. And its economic roots are deep in fishing, timber and agriculture.

But Bandon also has a tradition of hospitality that stretches back to the early part of this century, when visitors were forced to travel several days on rough wagon roads to reach this coastal village. In the old days, they came to escape the summer heat of the interior valleys, cool off in the morning fog that often descends on Bandon in the summer months, and frolic on the sunny beaches in the afternoon, after the fog had burned away.

Visitors still flock to Bandon in the summer for the same reasons, but now the little town has extended its appeal to the other seasons as well. Local boosters like to say Bandon has all the charm of a New England fishing village—but better sunsets.

The beaches near Bandon are a big part of its attractiveness. Every inch of Oregon's coastline is public— the legacy of a far-sighted governors and legislatures in 1913 and 1967—and Bandon boasts one of the most scenic stretches of beach along the entire Oregon coast. The beaches are easy to reach from several public access points along Beach Loop Drive or from the jetty that extends from the river mouth. The coastline is graced with an array of massive rocks and seastacks, weathered and pounded by the ocean into fantastic shapes. At low tide, the rocks and tidepools that shelter marine life can turn a simple beach walk into a expedition of discovery.

For its size, Bandon offers a surprisingly diverse choice of accommodations, ranging from a luxury resort with a golf course to an inexpensive youth hostel. There are also many no-frills motel rooms available, most with

Fog shrouds fishing boats at dawn in a harbor on Oregon's south coast.
DIANE KELSAY

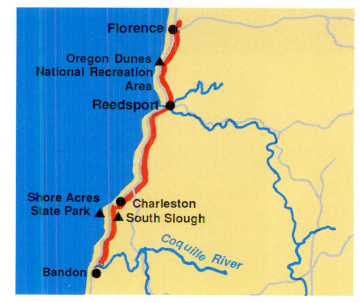

Above: Bandon's boat basin and the estuary of the Coquille River, as seen from Old Town. MARK HOY
Right: ANDREW E. CIER

easy beach access. My favorite alternative is the Spindrift Bed & Breakfast, run by Robbie Smith from her home on Beach Loop Drive. She and her husband, Don, who retired after many years as the head librarian at Washington State University, came to live in Bandon-by-the-sea after many years on the broad prairie of the Palouse country. They decided to take in guests so they could share their love and knowledge of the Oregon coastline. Since Don's death, Robbie has learned to appreciate the companion-ship of her guests even more, serving them elegant breakfasts and initiating them into the mysteries of agate hunting along the beach.

Although she enjoys her busy summers in Bandon, Robbie's true love is the winter season and the big storms

it brings. "The wind and the driving rain," she recalls appreciatively, "and the waves crashing right up towards the house on a high tide—it's really quite exciting. Then when the storm dies down, we all rush down to search the beach for agates and glass Japanese floats." The best of her finds lay scattered around the living room, a treasure trove of colored stones and glass for her guests to inspect before they gaze out the big plate-glass windows at another sunset on seastacks and windswept beach.

Another drawing card for Bandon is Old Town, a refurbished waterfront business district near the boat basin. It's a delightfully eccentric collection of practical and whimsical shops. In Old Town, you can buy motor oil at the hardware store, then cross the street and browse through fine art at just one of several tasteful galleries. There's a bakery, a well known cranberry candy maker (Bandon is the center of Oregon's cranberry growing region), a bookstore featuring New Age reading material, a wine-tasting room, the Bandon Historical Society Museum (with another gallery next door), and several shops that showcase the exquisite crafts made by local artisans.

Hugh and Ruth Harrison are two of the many Bandon residents who have made Old Town a success. Several years ago they left California to retire in Bandon—but their "retirement" has been anything but quiet. They've been instrumental in starting several businesses in Old Town and currently run a successful art gallery. They also built a 385-seat multipurpose arts and entertainment facility called Harbor Hall, which doubles as a community meeting center. And the Harrisons don't consider themselves remarkable in Bandon, where civic pride among the 2,500 residents is a way of life.

Bandon's selection of eating establishments is also a pleasant surprise for visitors who equate small-town dining with hamburger stands and greasy-spoon cafes. One of the most special restaurants is Andrea's, an Old Town fixture whose roots go back to the wave of urban counterculture refugees who arrived here in the 1970s. Andrea Gatov's comfortable atmosphere and homey style of cooking have evolved over the years, staying in step with current trends toward light meals prepared from the freshest foods. Fresh local seafood and homegrown lamb usually are featured, but the recipes can range from an elegant French sauce to a spicy Cajun roux. Fresh soups with homemade bread or muffins make for hearty lunches at Andrea's, too.

If you're lucky, you may arrive in Bandon during one of its many festivals. Memorial Day marks the Wine and Seafood Festival, while Fourth of July fireworks and other festivities highlight a patriotic midsummer celebration. In September, the Cranberry Festival focuses interest on the harvest of this area's most distinctive crop. In winter, the Bandon Storm Watchers gather to revel in the wind and waves, as well as for weekly lectures about the natural history of the south coast. And after deciding that you can never have too many festivals, Bandon's townspeople recently initiated another—the Christmas-time Festival of Lights.

Heading a few miles north from Bandon on U.S. 101, take the turnoff west on Seven Devils Road and follow signs pointing the way to the South Slough National Estuarine Reserve. Despite its important-sounding name, South Slough (pronounced *slew*) is a very low-key, but

Rocky headlands are eroded by the relentless pounding of the surf, an event celebrated by the Bandon Storm Watchers. CHARLIE BORLAND

Above: The receding tide exposes productive mudflats at the South Slough National Estuarine Reserve. © GARY BRAASCH

Right: A bald eagle, perched in a snag, watches for a meal on the tidal flats. KENNAN WARD

fascinating, area where learning and exploration go hand in hand. South Slough isn't set up as a tourist attraction—the primary purpose of this state-run installation is to support scientific research on the ecology of ocean estuaries—but a stop at South Slough's visitor center provides a pleasant side trip and adds a whole new appreciation for Oregon's coastal estuaries.

The new, half-million-dollar visitor center has a million-dollar view. It's perched on a hill high above South Slough, the name given to the estuary formed by a series of narrow arms of Coos Bay. The bay itself is the largest natural harbor between San Francisco and Seattle, and is a bustling seaport that exports lumber products all over the world. Because of the dedicated efforts of many local people, South Slough has been preserved from industrial development and was established in 1974 as the first sanctuary in a national program.

Inside the visitor center, you'll learn that estuaries are one of the most productive life zones. Their unique blend of salt water flowing in on the tides and fresh water bubbling down from the streams in the surrounding forests provides a womb-like environment, nurturing the wide variety of plants and animals that thrive there. Unfortunately, many of our most productive estuaries are being destroyed by industrial development—as has occurred in other parts of Coos Bay. That's why scientists come to South Slough to study how fish and other creatures utilize the area.

The best way to explore this intertidal zone is by canoe. If you don't happen to have one along, they can be rented at the head of South Slough in the little town of Charleston. My canoe tour was guided by John Garner, South Slough's education specialist at that time. As his long arms and efficient paddle strokes made short work of the distance across the slough, John explained that in a quiet, shallow-draft canoe, a visitor can approach birds and wild animals in South Slough more closely, as well as cruise the shallow tidal flats with relative ease. He added that it's a good idea to consult a tide chart or have an experienced guide along. Otherwise, you might be left high—and very soggy—on a mudflat when the tide goes out.

During our visit, John and I watched an oysterman harvesting shellfish. We floated past a herd of elk grazing in the meadows near the slough and spied a bald eagle

perched in a tall snag, watching for a meal out on the mudflats. John explained how important it is that visitors at South Slough get down and experience the web of life on the mudflats first hand. As part of his job, he leads several groups of school children down the nature trail from the visitor center every week to teach them about the ecology of the estuary. "That's our best hope in the future for

saving these areas" says John. "The children." A short drive north from South Slough takes you to Charleston, a fishing village. In season, fresh ocean fish—salmon, ling cod, albacore tuna, halibut and others—are available in several local seafood stores and there's a good chance you'll get to talk to some of the commercial fishermen if you stop in for a meal at one of the local cafes.

The web of lifeforms in coastal estuaries produces some of the most fertile—and precious—areas on earth. © GARY BRAASCH

Above: Tidal zone near Shore Acres State Park. JOHN REDDY

Right: *A statue of a great blue heron stands poised in the formal Japanese gardens at Shore Acres State Park.* BOB HARVEY

Facing page: *The Oregon Dunes National Recreation Area encompasses the largest dune-covered plain on the West Coast. Its shifting landscape is constantly on the move.* GEORGE WUERTHNER

The road west from Charleston takes you along a scenic coastal drive and to three of Oregon's most distinctive state parks. Sunset Bay offers full camping facilities and a sandy beach with a fine ocean view. Shore Acres may be Oregon's most unusual state park, sheltering exquisite formal gardens on a high bluff above the shore. They're remnants of the estate of shipping and lumber magnate Louis Simpson. In the early part of this century, Simpson brought exotic plants here from all over the world, utilizing his fleet of merchant ships. After his mansion burned to the ground—twice—and Simpson lost his fortune, he donated the gardens to the state. As thousands of visitors each year will attest, his loss was Oregon's gain.

At Cape Arago, the grassy picnic area on the promontory offers a magnificent view of miles of coastline and a rocky offshore reef. Steep trails lead down to tide pools

teeming with marine life. Or you can watch seals and sea lions sunning themselves on the rocky islands offshore. Depending on the weather, Cape Arago can be either a wonderful spot for a sunny picnic or the perfect perch from which to watch a winter storm roll in off the Pacific Ocean.

To return to U.S. 101, you'll need to backtrack to Charleston and then follow signs through Coos Bay to the junction with the main highway. Heading north again, after crossing the bridge over Coos Bay you'll notice a series of large sand dunes on the ocean (west) side of the road. This is the state's only scenic attraction that's permanently on the move. The Oregon Dunes scuttle up and down and around—a little like the local Dungeness crabs—from season to season, often changing their shape from one good winter storm to the next. In this shifting landscape you might encounter a perfect, crystal-clear lake wedged between towering dunes on one visit, then find it gone without a trace the next time you pass through.

The Oregon Dunes National Recreation Area (NRA), a 32,000-acre stretch of protected coastal dunes, stretches from Coos Bay in the south to the town of Florence in the north. It's the largest dune-covered plain on the West Coast, but the area encompasses much more than just dunes. There are coastal rivers here that teem with salmon in the fall, salt marshes sheltering waterfowl of all kinds, and coastal forests of cedar, hemlock and coast pine that beckon to explorers.

Fine campgrounds and challenging hiking trails are scattered throughout the national recreation area. A visit to the Oregon Dunes NRA Headquarters in Reedsport, located halfway between Coos Bay and Florence, will not only equip you with good maps and detailed descriptions of campgrounds and hiking trails, but can also get you up to date on special seasonal attractions, including migrating gray whales offshore or the best low tides for clam digging.

The dunes provide picturesque scenery, but the real sense of discovery comes when you get off the main road and take time to hike through this sandy maze. Even though it's possible to arrange for a guided horseback ride through the dunes (especially beautiful by moonlight!) or rent a motorized dune buggy, a hike through the dunes provides the best chance to experience the area's delicate beauty.

In the proper season you might see flocks of wintering ducks and geese, an osprey (fish hawk) diving from a snag to snatch up a meal of trout, or shorebirds wheeling in formation along the beach like fighter jets. Before the wind blows them away, there's a chance to find the tracks of bobcat, coyote, deer, raccoon, or even a bear. But to find them, you've got to get out and search for the changes afoot in the Oregon Dunes.

Astoria and the North Coast

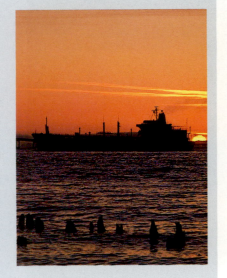

Above: *Huge freighters shoulder past Astoria's docks.*
ANDREW E. CIER
Right: *The beach and craggy headlands at Ecola State Park draw travelers from around the world.*
CHARLIE BORLAND

The north coast of Oregon features craggy headlands and long, sandy beaches that equal the splendor of the south coast. But the north coast has a more domesticated feel, with dairy farms nestled inland along the green river valleys and vacation homes of Willamette Valley residents clinging to hillsides and beaches along the coastline.

The crown jewel of the north coast must surely be the town of Astoria—America's oldest settlement west of the Rockies. Astoria watched from its perch on the low hills near the mouth of the Columbia River as an early trickle of fur trappers and explorers swelled into the steady stream of ocean freighters and fishing boats that surge past it on the river today.

Many Astoria families can trace their roots back to seafaring captains and crewmen, adventurers who crisscrossed the high seas trading furs and other bounty from

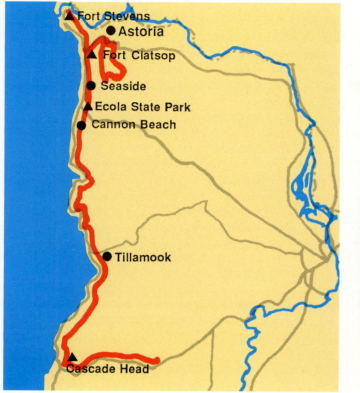

the Northwest. Some amassed great fortunes and built grand homes on Astoria's hillsides, where they could spend their time ashore scanning the river mouth for the first glimpse of incoming sailing ships.

With all that history behind them, Astorians might be content to preserve their 19th century architecture and the genteel traditions of that bygone era of great sailing ships and brave men. But they've managed to honor their past and still remain firmly rooted in the present. It's an attractive combination that keeps Astoria young.

Perhaps the excitement of the town's setting helps Astoria stay vibrant and alive, too. Nearby, waves crash over the dangerous bar where the broad Columbia River meets the Pacific Ocean. Hundreds of thousands of salmon and other ocean-going fish run up the Columbia past Astoria with the changing seasons, drawing large fleets of

commercial and sports fishermen. Huge freighters shoulder past Astoria's docks in a steady procession, to trade Oregon lumber and wheat at ports around the globe.

The best place to begin an exploration of Astoria is at Flavel House, on the corner of 8th and Duane streets, just off U.S. Highway 101. Once the grandest of Astoria's Victorian homes, it's now operated as a museum by the Clatsop County Historical Society.

Captain George Flavel built this imposing Queen Anne mansion on an entire city block near the heart of Astoria in 1885. Flavel obtained the first license to pilot ships across the dangerous Columbia bar in 1850 and managed to monopolize the trade. He retired in 1887, reputed to be the city's first millionaire.

Today, the Flavel mansion gives us a glimpse of the way the "other half" lived in a bygone era. The main floor

Above: *Flavel House, one of the grandest of Astoria's Victorian homes, is now a museum operated by the Clatsop County Historical Society.* CHARLIE BORLAND

rooms feature high ceilings, elegant woodwork and several original oil paintings, featuring the nautical themes admired by Captain Flavel. Each of the large rooms required a fireplace and each mantel piece was carved from a different exotic hardwood, accentuated by tiles imported from various ports in Asia and Europe. The three-story, octagonal tower on the northeast corner of the building overlooks the river, and the entire third floor of this massive home remains an unfinished ballroom (where visitors, unfortunately, are not permitted to venture).

While visiting Flavel House, pick up a pamphlet to guide you on a walking tour of historic homes in Astoria. It's a wonderful way to become intimately acquainted with the older sections of town. The guide includes so many fascinating stories about the families who constructed Astoria's old Victorian homes that it also serves as a useful primer on local history. Astoria often has been compared favorably to San Francisco, with its ornate restored Victorian houses—a comparison that causes many Astorians to bristle. After all, their hometown is older! But in both of these old seaports there's a renewed interest by the townspeople in the preservation and restoration of their beautiful Victorian homes. A walk along Astoria's Franklin Avenue—the route of the walking tour—reinforces the impression that Astoria's past is alive and well. At the corner of Franklin and 14th Street, the spirit lives on at the Rosebriar Inn, a bed and breakfast operated by Ann Leenstra and her sister, Judith Papendick. This rambling old home was built by local banker Frank Patton in 1902, about the time Astoria reached the pinnacle of its success as a center of salmon processing and ocean-going trade. In 1950, the building was purchased by the Catholic Church, which added an annex and converted it to a convent for 14 nuns.

Ann and Judith were living in the Portland area when they discovered the old Victorian house. According to Ann, it was "love at first sight," but they had no idea how much labor their love would involve. They stripped the walls and floors back to turn-of-the-century motifs, wallpapered each of the nun's rooms in keeping with the original style, and opened Astoria's first bed and breakfast in 1983. Since then, they've been joined by a half-dozen similar establishments and the bed and breakfast movement in Astoria's

Victorians is still going strong. No wonder—with such an inspiring setting and so many historic buildings, it's an ideal marriage of form and function.

Just down the hill from the Rosebriar Inn, writer Dave Hughes keeps his office in another historic building in Astoria's main business district. Hughes, the author of *An Angler's Astoria* and several other books, writes about fly fishing and other outdoor themes. A native Astorian, he also has some theories about his hometown.

"Astoria lives by its water," says Hughes, "but is defined by its hills. The layers of Astoria climb in patient fashion from the river to the top of the hill."

The hilltop most visitors will want to see is Coxcomb Hill, where the Astoria Column stands. Follow signs up a scenic, winding drive to the top, where this monument to Astoria was constructed in 1926. A frieze, depicting major events in Astoria's history, spirals around the column. From the column's observation deck, 166 steps up, you're treated to a panoramic view of the area surrounding Astoria's peninsula.

To the north, the graceful Astoria Bridge (also called the Trans-Columbia Bridge, or Columbia/Megler Bridge) spans 4.1 miles of the Columbia River, connecting U.S. 101 with the Washington side. The Columbia bar and nearby wave-washed beaches are clearly visible on the western horizon. To the south, the view extends across Young's Bay to Saddle Mountain, a popular hiking destination. Later, you might drive the loop south of the bay, up Young's River on State Route 202. It's a 30-mile round trip past wooded hills, dairy farms and Young's River Falls, a pleasant spot for a picnic or other family outing.

After you've visited the Astoria Column, you can experience the city's "bottom layer" with a walking tour of the waterfront. Follow signs to the Columbia River Maritime Museum, at the foot of 17th Street, where you park your car. An old railroad line parallels the waterfront and serves as your footpath access to the docks. But you'll have to exercise some caution, because this is an active waterfront—watch out for trucks and machinery. You will discover pilot boat docks, marine equipment stores, restaurants and specialty shops tucked into the wharf. Take your time—this is an opportunity to see and hear the working side of Astoria.

Above: *Astoria "lives by its water, but is defined by its hills."*
© GARY BRAASCH

Left: *The Astoria Bridge carries U.S. 101 4.1 miles across the Columbia River between Washington and Oregon.* CHARLIE BORLAND

Facing page: *Saddle Mountain offers a challenging hike, as well as fine views of the Oregon Coast Range.* CHARLIE BORLAND

But don't miss the Maritime Museum, one of Astoria's highlights. Established in 1962 to preserve the maritime heritage of the Columbia River basin and the north coast area, it's now recognized as one of the finest maritime collections on the West Coast. The museum's new building is equally impressive—a swooping, modernistic structure that gives the impression of a wave breaking on the river's edge.

Inside, you'll immediately enter the Great Hall, an open, airy space that houses a collection of several small fishing boats and a restored, 25-foot Coast Guard surf rescue boat. The remainder of the museum is divided into distinctive galleries, with collections ranging from a scale model of the *Tonquin,* an early sailing ship that explored the Northwest coastline, to the working bridge and pilot house of the destroyer USS *Knapp.* The galleries house a wealth of historic artifacts gleaned from shipwrecks, salmon canneries and native villages. For some hands-on history, take the helm of the schooner *Forrester* or peer through a real submarine periscope.

Docked outside the Maritime Museum is its largest exhibit, the lightship *Columbia*. This 128′ vessel was the last lightship to serve on the West Coast. Stationed at the mouth of the Columbia, its 600,000-candlepower light warned incoming ships of the dangerous crossing ahead. As part of the Maritime Museum's admission price, visitors can board the retired lightship and inspect the crew's areas below.

Lewis and Clark's famous overland expedition first sighted the Pacific Ocean at a point across the river from what would later become Astoria, and they wintered south of the future townsite. Fort Clatsop, the log structure built by the expedition members to shelter their party from the rain of that 1805-1806 coastal Oregon winter, has been reconstructed and is now maintained as a national memorial.

A few miles south of Astoria, the access road from U.S. Highway 101 to Fort Clatsop passes through thick stands of hemlock and Sitka spruce trees, with understory shrubs that complete a wall of nearly impenetrable cover. In summer, the countryside looks verdant and alive. In winter, the season of arrival for Lewis and Clark's party of 33 explorers, the thick foliage often combines with fog and rain to isolate the area from the rest of the world. The expedition party members reported intense feelings of homesickness, as well as various other real aches and fevers, during their damp winter at Fort Clatsop. It rained on all but 12 of the 106 days they spent there.

At the Fort Clatsop visitor center, excellent displays of expedition artifacts, a slide program and a film on the Lewis and Clark journey are supplemented in summer with living history. Park rangers in authentic costumes fire muzzleloader muskets, carve a functional canoe from a single spruce log, or reenact other survival skills essential to the explorers. The recreated fort—cramped, dank and smoky—provides a glimpse of the dreary daily routine they endured. A trail leads down to the canoe landing on the Lewis and Clark River (renamed in their honor) where they first landed to select a site for their winter quarters.

Storm fronts often provide dramatic lighting along the Oregon coast, as in this scene near Cannon Beach.
ANDREW E. CIER

Nearby, Fort Stevens State Park provides a good base of operations for visits to Fort Clatsop and the nearby beaches. Open year-round, Fort Stevens has more than 600 campsites, including facilities for recreational vehicles. A network of trails for hiking or biking connects the campgrounds with the beach, where you can inspect the rusting hulk of the *Peter Iredale,* an English four-masted sailing ship that was driven aground by a winter storm in 1906. There's also an elevated observation platform, a fine vantage point for watching waves batter the long, rocky

jetty extending out from the mouth of the Columbia River—the Great River of the West that Lewis and Clark were sent to explore.

Fort Stevens originally was a military fort, built during the Civil War. Although the post closed in 1947, you can tour a museum, as well as Fort Stevens' gun emplacements, which were the only mainland U.S. installations fired on—by a Japanese submarine—during World War II.

When you leave Astoria, there's still plenty of exploration to be done along U.S. 101 as you drive south. The north coast is home to a series of state parks that collectively rank among the most scenic in the world. They are all well worth exploring—especially if you fancy beautiful beaches and long ocean vistas.

You can follow U.S. 101 south from Astoria to Seaside, or take the slower county road along the Lewis and Clark River as a scenic alternative. The thriving little town of Seaside has a long history as a coastal resort and today still draws thousands of visitors from the Portland area in the summer. Its Promenade provides a lovely beach-side walk and numerous boutiques and amusement halls that cluster along the shoreline. However, Seaside is predominantly a "tourist town" and ought to be considered more of a people attraction than a scenic attraction. A few miles to the south, Cannon Beach also caters to visitors, but manages to maintain its original charm. A thriving artists' colony, Cannon Beach boasts small, unique shops and galleries, fine restaurants, and distinctive oceanside resorts. It's also blessed with a dramatic location. Ponderous Haystack Rock graces the beach, flanked by smaller seastacks known as The Needles, while steep, tree-clad hillsides provide a framing backdrop on the east edge of town.

Ecola State Park covers 1,300 acres of shoreline between Seaside and Cannon Beach, where the park's access road begins. Beautiful beaches, fine hiking trails and some of Oregon's most dramatic ocean scenery make Ecola Park stand a notch above others nearby—as more than 200,000 annual visitors can testify. Views of Tillamook Rock and its abandoned lighthouse provide the scenic raw material for artistic creations by visiting amateur and professional photographers.

From Cannon Beach south on U.S. 101, a string of charming coastal villages and intriguing state parks

beckons to the visitor, but one stop stands out. The Tilla-mook Cheese Factory, just north of the town of Tillamook, produces one of Oregon's most popular exports. Here you can watch and learn about the cheese-making process, then snack on the results. Local dairy farms produce much of the milk for the many delightful cheeses and excellent ice cream made here.

South of Tillamook, U.S. 101 bends east, away from the ocean. A half-hour drive will bring you back to the shoreline near Cascade Head, a popular hiking area. The U.S. Forest Service has been studying the spruce-hemlock groves at Cascade Head since 1934 and the area is now designated a Scenic Research Area. It offers views of the Salmon River estuary to the south, as well as showy wildflower displays in the spring on the broad meadows near the ocean.

Just a few miles south of Cascade Head is the junc-tion of U.S. 101 with State Route 18, a scenic route east through the Coast Range that will take you to the heart of Oregon's thriving new wine region.

Tillamook Head rises abruptly between the coastal villages of Seaside and Cannon Beach. The headland also shelters one of the state's most popular parks, Ecola State Park. CHARLIE BORLAND

Wineries of the Willamette Valley

Above: The foundation of Oregon's new wine industry: pinot noir grapes ready for harvest. DIANE KELSAY
Right: Vineyards in the rolling hills of the Willamette Valley have produced vintages in recent years that compare favorably with the red wines of Burgundy. CHARLIE BORLAND

There's something inherently attractive about a wine-growing region. Perhaps it's the romance of fine wine. Or the pastoral beauty of the countryside where most vineyards thrive. Whatever the reason, winery tours have become popular with many visitors to Europe and California, especially the latter, where the Napa Valley has become the second-most-popular tourist destination in the state—right behind Disneyland.

By international standards, Oregon's wine districts have a long way to go. But in the eyes of wine experts, local growers and the visitors who already have discovered this hidden treasure, they're already there. California has the quantity—in both total number of visitors and total volume of wine. (California produces almost a thousand gallons of wine for every gallon produced by an Oregon winery.) But Oregon wineries have achieved something far more elusive: quality—and the rest of the world is beginning to take note. One well known California wine writer recently called Oregon's pinot noir "the blue-eyed wine right now." And a California distributor paid Oregon wines the ultimate compliment, saying the only thing wrong with them was that "there's not enough to go around." At an International Pinot Noir Celebration held in Oregon, Robert Drouhin, head of the prestigious Joseph Drouhin winery in Burgundy, France, compared Oregon wineries to those in his home region: "The structure of the wineries here, the family approach, is like Burgundy. They are not big investors. It is not easy to start from scratch, as they did. It was courageous."

Perhaps the most courageous of them all was David Lett, sometimes called the "godfather of Oregon pinot noir." Lett came to the Willamette Valley in 1966, freshly graduated from the enology program (the study of wines and wine making) at the University of California at Davis. His professors had warned him that fine wines couldn't be grown in Oregon's Willamette Valley—it simply was too rainy and cold.

But Lett had other ideas. He studied climatological records of the area for the past 50 years and thought he saw a pattern that reminded him of northern France. Besides, Oregon farmers had grown wonderful fruits and berries for more than a century—the mild Willamette Valley climate seemed ideal for growing almost everything.

Most of all, Lett had very definite ideas about the pinot noir grape, the source of the great wines of Burgundy. In California's sunny climate, pinot noir grapes flourished, but grew so fast and matured so quickly that the resulting wine was uniformly mediocre. In Burgundy's climate, the pinot noir vines struggled through uneven growing seasons—conditions that were often marginal for their development. The resulting wines could be complete failures one year and a spectacular vintage the next.

"I felt comfortable with the French idea that for a wine to develop character, the grape must have had to struggle," says Lett. His ideas proved prophetic, not only for the pinot noir wines, but also for the budding Oregon wine industry itself. After two decades of struggle, the pinot noirs made by Lett and other Oregon winemakers have been judged the equal—and in some years superior—to the great wines of Burgundy in recent blind tastings.

There are now more than 65 wineries in Oregon, the majority clustered in the hilly farm country of the Willamette Valley between Portland and Salem. Lett's Eyrie

Vineyards is near McMinnville, where Lett continues to experiment with the processing of new grape varieties and new "clones" of pinot noir vines in the turkey processing plant he converted to a winery. Lett still considers wine "his mistress"—so much so that he keeps a cot in a corner of the winery, so he can get up in the middle of the night to check his French oak barrels during particularly critical times.

Lett's Eyrie Vineyards welcomes the public only at a special Thanksgiving weekend open house, so our tour of

Left: *An Oregon pinot noir "blush" wine provides the perfect complement for a picnic lunch.* CHARLIE BORLAND

Above: Oak barrels rest quietly while the wine inside matures and gains character. DIANE KELSAY
Right: Large stainless steel vats are cooled to the perfect temperature for fermentation in the early stages of wine processing. DIANE KELSAY/BOB HARVEY

the Oregon wine districts must be directed to other wineries. They present a wide variety from which to choose.

The best way to plan your tour is to get the pamphlet "Discover Oregon Wineries," put out by the Oregon Winegrowers Association (see the Sources chapter for details.) You'll find Oregon wineries grouped into seven different tours, four in the Willamette Valley.

Some of the smaller wineries have no full-time tasting facilities, but are happy to receive guests if you contact them ahead of time. The larger wineries maintain tasting rooms and regular schedules for your convenience.

Southwest of Portland and just south of the little town of Dundee, signs along U.S. Highway 99W point to an access road running northwest up the hill to Sokol Blosser Winery. One of the largest wineries in Oregon, Sokol Blosser (the name is a combination of the names of the two families who own and operate the winery) recently opened its new tasting room and gift shop in a shady grove of trees on an airy hilltop. Inside, large windows look out over the vineyards and in summer the picnic area outside offers a similar view of the hilly vineyard country nearby. Sokol Blosser produces an impressive variety of fine wines, including white riesling, chardonnay, pinot noir, merlot, gewurztraminer, sauvignon blanc, Müller-Thurgau and three special blends. Most of these wines are available daily for tasting.

Before continuing our tour, it's best to say a few words about the labeling of Oregon wines. The state's winemakers were instrumental in enacting some of the strictest labeling laws in the world for their wines—another blow for quality! Oregon wines can be labeled only on the basis of the type of grape(s) in the wine, so no French districts, such as Chablis or Burgundy, appear in the names. There are also strict rules regarding the percentage of a grape variety that must be included in a wine before it can carry that name, as well as the percentage of grapes from a certain year's harvest that must be used before the vintage year can be noted on the label.

A few miles north on U.S. 99W in Dundee, you'll find the Knudsen Erath Winery, one of the largest wineries in Oregon (its tasting room was closed as of this writing). In a state area where all the wineries are small, "largest" does not connote a drop in quality—far from it. Knudsen Erath produces a full line of reasonably-priced fine wines. In addition to excellent pinot noir, chardonnay and white riesling, they produce several blends of their varieties. To visit the Knudsen Erath winery, follow signs northwest from Dundee on 9th St., which turns into Worden Hill Rd. The tasting room at the winery perches on a steep hill and features outdoor tables for those who bring their own bread and cheese to enjoy along with the wine.

If you backtrack south on U.S. 99W past the little town of Lafayette, you will see signs pointing north on a county road to Chateau Benoit. This winery also is sited on a hilltop, with fine views of the surrounding countryside, although the concrete building itself is unimpressive and so new that the trees haven't had a chance to grow up to provide summer shade. However, winemaker Rich Cushman offers a wide variety of wines, including pinot noir, riesling, chardonnay, Müller-Thurgau, sauvignon blanc and a white pinot noir called Rainbow Run.

In addition, Chateau Benoit is one of the few Oregon wineries that produces sparkling wine, Brut and Blanc de Blanc. (Sparkling wines are known in many wine-growing regions as champagne, but Oregon's strict labeling laws don't allow use of that district name.) Although sparkling wines require a great deal of time and extra equipment, many Oregon winemakers believe the region will eventually produce some great ones, since the pinot noir and chardonnay grapes grown here are also the predominant varieties used in classic French champagnes.

At the southern end of the Willamette Valley, near Eugene, another Oregon wine district is emerging. There are currently three established wineries in this region and several small newcomers. Hinman Vineyards is the largest of the group and can be reached by driving southwest

Above: Even though the climate in the Willamette Valley is mild, grapevines often struggle through uneven growing seasons. The resulting wines can exhibit more "character" than those grown under ideal conditions.
Left: A winery worker cleans a stainless steel tank in preparation for wine fermentation. Because many Oregon wineries are quite new, they often employ the most recent winemaking technology. DIANE KELSAY PHOTOS

Above: *David Smith and Doyle Hinman sample the most recent vintage from their winery, Hinman Vineyards, near Eugene.*
Right: *Grapes are unloaded at harvest time, en route to a machine that crushes the fruit and filters out stems and skins.* DIANE KELSAY PHOTOS

from Eugene on the Lorane Highway and following signs west from the junction at Spencer Creek Road.

Doyle Hinman and his partner, David Smith, have recently completed a half-million-dollar renovation of their winery, enabling them to double their production. With his winery already the second largest in the state, Hinman has his sights set clearly on becoming number one. A brash newcomer by comparison to old hands such as David Lett, Hinman understands that the Oregon wine industry is in a state of flux. "You know," he says as he sits in his shiny new glass-and-brick tasting room, "this place was nothing but dirt just a few years ago. We really do personify change around here."

Hinman's success is based on an approach different from that of most Oregon wineries, who have staked their futures on the production of high-priced, vintage wines. Although Hinman Vineyards produces some fine vintages of pinot noir, chardonnay and cabernet sauvignon wines, Doyle has taken his insistence on quality one step further—in the volume production of medium-priced white and "blush" wines, sometimes called picnic wines, from riesling and pinot noir grapes. Between the wine coolers and the bottles of pinot noir that sell for $15 a bottle and up, Hinman has found his niche.

Doyle is also an innovator in the marketing of Oregon wine. Despite grumbles from traditionalists, his was one of the first Oregon wineries to package wine for bulk customers, such as large restaurants, in the new plastic bag-in-a-box containers. He hasn't forsaken the traditional wine bottle, just moved beyond it. As a result, Hinman wines can be found as the "house wines" in many of Oregon's finest restaurants and are beginning to receive wider distribution in other states.

"We haven't won as many awards as some of the other Oregon wineries," Hinman admits, "but the notoriety that's important to me is the satisfaction that our winery is growing and people obviously like our wines." Even with the rapid growth rate of Hinman's wine sales, the atmosphere here is placid. The new tasting room and patio provide a relaxing spot to sip some of Hinman Vineyard's finest, while gazing over the neatly-tended vines below.

Near Hinman Vineyards, take Territorial Road north to Forgeron Vineyard, near the little town of Elmira. The

tasting room here is open all week from June through September and on weekends during the winter months. Fine pinot noir, cabernet sauvignon, chardonnay, and white riesling wines can be tasted.

A few more miles north on Territorial Road is the junction with U.S. 99W, at the little town of Monroe.

Follow signs to Alpine Vineyards, known for its estate-bottled pinot noir, chardonnay, riesling, gewurztraminer and cabernet sauvignon wines. Check the "Discover Oregon Wineries" pamphlet for tasting room hours. As with many of the Oregon wineries you choose to visit, you'll find that here, small is best.

An exciting new era is dawning for Hinman Vineyards and the entire Oregon wine industry. DIANE KELSAY

The Coastal Cascades

Waldo Lake
Breitenbush Hot Springs
McKenzie River

Above: DIANE KELSAY
Right: *Mt. Jefferson from Scout Lake: an alpine portrait in all its splendor.*
CHARLIE BORLAND

The Cascade Range forms the heart of what most visitors look for when they visit Oregon. Snow-capped volcanic peaks, like Mount Hood, draped at the flanks with unbroken forests of big, green fir trees; countless rushing brooks, waterfalls and still mountain lakes; deer, elk, beaver and trout—all are part of this alpine portrait.

It's an attractive picture. All the elements of alpine splendor can be found in the Cascades, although not necessarily everywhere at the same time. And to find the best parts of this mountain puzzle, you do have to get off the most-traveled routes, of course!

The Cascade Range marks a dividing line between the wet western valleys of the state—the rainy image most outsiders identify with Oregon—and the high, dry plateaus of Eastern Oregon. The Cascades form an effective barrier to moist storms blowing off the Pacific Ocean, pulling down their moisture in the forms of rain and snow, and creating a rainshadow that extends for several hundred miles inland to the east, effectively parching that region and transforming it into a high desert.

The effect of all that water on the Cascade Range is dramatic. Much of the rain and melting snow filters down through porous volcanic soils, providing a water reserve in underground springs and high mountain lakes, ensuring that Oregon's famous river systems will run cold and clear through the dry summer and fall seasons.

All that moisture also grows big trees. The first white explorers in Oregon discovered groves of Douglas fir that were impressive indeed, with tree trunks wider than a man was tall and crowns that intercepted the sun's rays hundreds of feet above the forest floor. The forests of those trees blanketed so many miles that it seemed a man never could cut down enough of them to make a dent in the canopy.

Now, after more than a century of intensive logging, many people can see the day when all the big, old trees will be logged, replaced by neat rows of the "factory trees" produced by reforestation. Fortunately, some of the biggest old-growth trees have been preserved in official wilderness areas. Others, which eventually may be logged, are easy to find along the route through the Cascades that I'll describe in this chapter. From Salem, Oregon's state capital, take State Route 22 east toward Detroit Lake. Near the village of Shaw, State Route 214 leads east toward Silver Falls State Park. This is Oregon's largest state park, featuring an amazing variety of waterfalls that tumble off forested canyon walls.

Back on State Route 22, the road follows the North Santiam River Valley through rolling farmland and gradually gains altitude as it crosses the foothills of the Cascades. At the little town of Detroit, you will see a large, man-made lake, formed when the North Santiam River was dammed.

Near Detroit, find the sign for the paved Forest Service road leading north to Breitenbush Springs. Here an old hot springs resort has been restored. The old lodge now is open and visitors can rent cabins, "take the waters," and enjoy the peacefulness and healing powers of their surroundings.

The old-growth forest surrounding the hot springs provides a fine setting for cross-country skiing in winter and hiking into nearby wilderness areas in summer. When

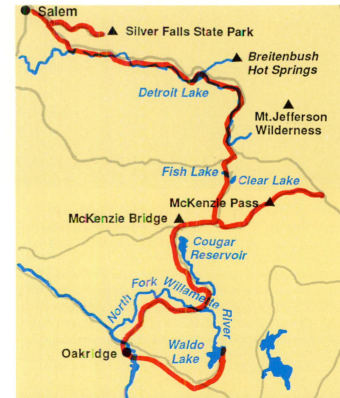

Above: *Silver Creek in Silver Falls State Park, where an amazing variety of waterfalls tumble down forested canyons.* CHARLIE BORLAND

Mt. Jefferson blocks a storm front approaching from the west.
DAVID JENSEN

you return from your exertions, a long soak in the hot springs soothes aching muscles. Only vegetarian meals—but hearty, tasty ones—are served at Breitenbush and the cabin facilities are quite simple and rustic.

Route 22 turns south past Detroit, paralleling the crest of the Cascade Range and passing through impressive stands of big Douglas firs. The state highway department works hard to keep this road free of ice and snow during the winter, but it can be treacherous driving, especially after a big storm. Check road conditions with the state Highway Patrol before attempting a winter passage.

In warmer seasons, be sure to note several good access points on the east side of the road, into the Mt. Jefferson Wilderness Area. This is one of the state's best-known wilderness areas, offering spectacular mountain scenery, profuse wildflower displays in spring, and several climbing routes up the mountain. Because of its popularity, it is best to avoid the Mt. Jefferson area on holiday weekends.

At the junction with U.S. Highway 20, turn west and travel 4 miles to the junction with State Route 126. Turn south on Route 126, following signs for the Eugene/Springfield area.

You are now traversing a lava flow that is quite young geologically—some sections were covered by an eruption just 1,600 years ago. It's a graphic reminder that the whole Cascade Range still is volcanically active. Of course, anyone who remembers the eruption of Mt. St. Helens in 1981 needs no reminder.

After a short drive you will see signs for Fish Lake campground on the west side of the road. Just past Fish Lake, a sign marks the turnoff east for the Santiam Wagon Road Trailhead of the McKenzie River National Recreation Trail. This trail parallels the river for the next 26.5 miles, with 11 parking areas scattered along Highway 126 providing excellent access.

The McKenzie River Trail gets you off the highway and into this beautiful Cascades canyon. The McKenzie, famed for its good rainbow trout fishing and exciting white-water rafting, is a major tributary in the Willamette River system. The river begins at Clear Lake, a mile below the upper trailhead. Clear Lake was formed when the channel of the McKenzie was blocked by lava flows just 3,000 years ago. Trees killed by the rising water have been preserved in a ghost forest on the lake bottom and still can be easily observed, providing an eerie attraction for hikers and boaters.

Several large waterfalls are highlights along the trail route, including Sahalie Falls, where the river water drops more than 100' straight down into a large pool. At Tamolitch, the McKenzie actually disappears through the porous lava, leaving a dry river bed except during flood periods, when the channel refills and water drops precipitously over a 60' cliff.

There are four campgrounds along the McKenzie River Trail, so it's feasible to carry a backpack and camp as you go. The canyon is especially beautiful in the fall season, when vine maple and other hardwoods color the canyon walls with reds and yellows. Fishing in the McKenzie River and its tributaries is also at its best in late summer and early fall. If you plan to hike long sections of the trail, be sure to wear sturdy boots, as the rough lava flows are

hard on shoes. The lower 10 to 12 miles of the trail often remain free of snow in winter and can be enjoyed year-round.

Near the lower end of the McKenzie River National Recreation Trail is the highway junction of Route 126 and Route 242. Also known as the Old McKenzie Pass Highway, State Route 242 is a winding, scenic road. It leads east, up through an old-growth fir forest, then cuts across dense stands of lodgepole pine, and finally traverses a rugged lava field before dropping down on the east side of the Cascades near the little town of Sisters.

At the top of McKenzie Pass on Route 242 is Dee Wright Observatory. From the deck of this observatory you can scan 75 square miles of lava fields and, when the

Recent lava flows abound near the Cascades summit, an area of ongoing vulcanism. North and Middle Sister Mountains in the background. CHARLIE BORLAND

weather is clear, sight down the line of Cascade volcanoes from Mt. Hood in the north to the Three Sisters in the south. This route is not maintained in winter, and becomes a challenging cross-country ski course when the highway gates are closed after the first big snow of the season.

Return to Route 126 and continue west through the little town of McKenzie Bridge. Near the river crossing, the Log Cabin Inn, a restored roadhouse, offers a surprisingly broad selection of home-style meals. Venison and trout are specialties. Continue downstream (west) on Route 126 and, just before you reach the little town of Blue River, find the turnoff to the south for Forest Service Road 19, sometimes called Aufderheide Drive. This paved forest road takes you past Cougar Reservoir, up the South Fork of the McKenzie River, over a saddle at about 4,000′ of altitude and down the valley of the North Fork of the Willamette River to the junction with State Route 58 near the town of Oakridge. (This is another road not maintained by snow-removal crews in winter, so check conditions with the Forest Service ranger station in Blue River or the ranger station in Oakridge before setting out.)

This route will give you an intimate look at the variety of river and lake country on the west side of the Cascades. There are several undeveloped (no hookups) campgrounds along the way for self-contained trailers or tents. The French Pete extension of Three Sisters Wilderness, home to some of the largest Douglas firs remaining in the Cascades, borders Road 19 on the east side and there are several good trail access points into the wilderness. Fishing in Cougar Reservoir, as well as the two rivers paralleled by the road and several nearby alpine lakes, is outstanding for rainbow, brook and cutthroat trout.

The North Fork of the Willamette River offers a particularly scenic canyon drive that's overlooked by most visitors. This stream was the subject of statewide interest a few years ago, when a local utility company tried to get approval to build several hydroelectric projects in the canyon. Citizens responded by supporting passage of a bill in the state legislature that made the North Fork a State Scenic Waterway and effectively prohibited further dam-building on the river. The North Fork of the Willamette is a fly-fishing-only stream along almost its entire length, so anglers should be careful to use the right equipment.

At the junction of Road 19 with State Route 58, turn east, proceed through the town of Oakridge and continue on Route 58 for approximately 25 miles until you reach Waldo Lake Road, Forest Service Road 5897. This road also is closed by snow in winter, but after the snow has melted (usually late June) you can drive approximately 6 miles to Waldo Lake, where three large campgrounds grace the lake's eastern shoreline.

Waldo Lake is high, wild and crystal clear. The water in this 10-mile-long lake at the crest of the Cascade Range is so transparent that rock features more than a hundred feet down are clearly visible. A few years ago, scientists studying water quality found something startling about Waldo Lake. Their tests showed that, in terms of purity, the water from Waldo Lake compares favorably with lab-grade distilled water.

Because of these revelations, conservationists succeeded in having the land on the north and west side of Waldo Lake preserved as the Waldo Wilderness Area, to protect the watershed from damage by logging or other

Above: *The French Pete Wilderness Area holds some of the largest old-growth Douglas fir trees remaining in the Cascades, and a verdant plant community made possible by the big trees.* © GARY BRAASCH

Facing page: *The McKenzie River, a tributary of the Willamette River system, is famed for its rainbow trout fishing and whitewater rafting.* GEORGE WUERTHNER

Waldo Lake is high and wild, its water crystal clear and perfectly pure. DAVE SWAN

development. But the three large developed campgrounds on the lake's eastern shoreline offer the visitor a base of operations from which to explore the splendor of this high-altitude basin by foot or by boat.

When Waldo Lake's largest outlet stream, the North Fork of the Willamette, was designated a State Scenic Waterway, legislators decided to include Waldo Lake in the designation, making it the first lake in Oregon so honored.

I visited the lake with Andy Kerr, who works for Oregon Natural Resources Council, Oregon's largest conservation group. We spent the day canoeing the big lake and hiking. That night we decided to take advantage of a bright full moon and again launched our canoe. We weren't quite prepared for what we found, however. Waldo Lake's water is so clear that our canoe appeared to be floating in space, suspended between the rocky bottom—which looked near enough to touch—and the moonlit sky.

So impressive was this phenomenon that Andy and I were both rendered speechless—especially remarkable for Andy, who's accustomed to regaling congressional committees and packed meeting halls at speaking events. After a while, it didn't even seem right to disturb the surface of the lake, so we stopped paddling and just drifted. It was an unforgettable experience.

Waldo Lake seems to make a strong impression on many of its visitors. Even though there are plenty of things to do on or around the lake, a surprising number of people just sit and watch this big body of water for hours on end. When its water is calm, the lake seems to exert a soothing effect on the soul. At midday, when the wind usually whistles up through the pass, waves begin to crash on the rocky shoreline. That's become my favorite time to sit back and watch the power of Waldo Lake.

Mid-day has become a favorite time for sailors, too. Sailboating and windsurfing have increased in popularity at Waldo as visitors began to pass the word. Boats with motors are allowed on the lake, but must keep their speed below 10 miles per hour. Sailboats, of course, have no speed limit and can be seen racing with the wind through the fine mountain scenery. It's usually advisable to keep a canoe off the water at midday when the wind is blowing, but mornings and evenings are perfect times to paddle through the lake's many calm bays and rocky islands.

A good hiking trail rings the lake, tracing a 21-mile round trip that can be accomplished in one day if you're in good walking shape. But don't forget—Waldo Lake lies in a basin that's above 5,000' high in elevation, so the air is a little thinner than at sea level! Feeder trails lead off from the main trail into the lakes and basins of the Waldo Wilderness Area. Although the big lake doesn't have enough nutrients in its water to support a decent fish population, the nearby lakes and streams more than make up for it with healthy populations of trout. The only negative element at Waldo Lake is its legendary population of mosquitoes. Most of the high Cascades lakes are plagued by mosquitoes, but Waldo is ringed by small melt-off ponds that make perfect breeding grounds for the pesky critters. Consequently, even the most ardent admirers of Waldo Lake avoid the area during midsummer, from early July through mid-August.

During the rest of year—even in winter, when you must ski the six miles up the road to the lake—a trip to Waldo Lake is tonic. The crisp air, the clear water and the solitude—isn't this what those picture postcards of the Cascade Range really were trying to tell us?

A canoe is the perfect craft for exploring the rocky reefs and calm bays of big Waldo Lake. DAVE SWAN

The North Umpqua

Steamboat Inn
Umpqua Valley Wineries
Wildlife Safari

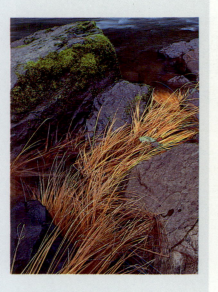

Above: *The North Umpqua River runs cold and clear from its source near Diamond Lake to its junction with the South Umpqua below Roseburg.* CHARLIE BORLAND **Right:** *A fly angler fighting a summer-run steelhead trout on the North Umpqua River.* MARK HOY **Facing page:** *A steelhead reluctantly waiting to be released by a lucky fly angler. Many anglers on the North Umpqua release their catches to ensure a healthy steelhead population in the future.*
DOUGLAS O'LOONEY

Fishing is one of the durable traditions that binds modern Northwesterners to their past. When native people first migrated to the region, they found an abundance of salmon and trout unrivaled anywhere in the world. The profusion of fish runs not only provided them with their primary food source, it also supplied an annual harvest pattern that marked the changing seasons and gave order to the people's lives.

For many Northwesterners today, the changing fishing seasons still order the passing of time. Although most anglers don't depend on fishing for their livelihoods anymore, fishing is still by far the most popular participant sport in the region. And even though fishing is no longer a matter of life and death, try convincing a Northwest fisherman of that!

Oregon has such a variety of fish and fishing locales that most fishers are content to sample just a fraction of the possibilities. The state boasts hundreds of clean, clear rivers—ranging in size from frothing mountain streams to the mighty Columbia River. Lakes run the gamut from huge man-made impoundments that support bass, landlocked salmon and trout, to tiny alpine lakes where only the smallest brook trout can survive.

Faced with so much diversity, some anglers prefer to specialize. And some are simply driven to find the most challenging fishing available and to succeed at it—to give themselves the ultimate test. That's what fishing the North Umpqua River is all about.

Most fishermen concede that fly fishing—where the angler limits himself to using artificial flies and casts an unweighted line to propel them—is the most technically demanding form of fishing. On the upper section of the North Umpqua River, the rules say "artificial flies only" and the quarry is summer steelhead, the ocean-going form of rainbow trout that's reputed to be one of the finest sport fish in the world.

Consider also that the North Umpqua is a cold, fast-moving Cascade river, with lots of wicked rapids and a slippery algae-covered bottom, so one false step can mean a fisherman will be swept downstream into rocky white water. Put it all together and you have the ultimate fishing challenge in Oregon.

The North Umpqua's challenge brings fly anglers from all over the world to fish the river. And the river's fame keeps spreading—by word of mouth between fishermen, and through more and more articles in fishing magazines and books. One writer even dubbed it "finishing school" for fly fishermen.

The summer steelhead are wonderfully powerful fish, having spent two or three, sometimes four years in the ocean feeding on shrimp and smaller fish. On the North Umpqua, they average eight pounds or more—and some weigh in at over 15 pounds. When hooked on fly-fishing equipment, they often explode out of the water, jumping several times before either breaking free or exhausting themselves in battle with the lucky angler. Along the North Umpqua, many anglers prefer to release the summer steelhead they catch, to allow the fish to swim upstream and spawn naturally in one of the river's tributaries.

Because steelhead are notoriously difficult to catch on a fly, even the best anglers spend hours of fishing time for every steelhead they land. And part of their reward for fishing the North Umpqua is the opportunity to experience

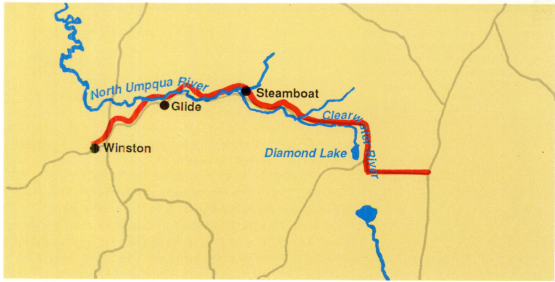

Diamond Lake, near the headwaters of the North Umpqua, offers excellent fishing for rainbow trout, as well as a resort and several campgrounds with modern facilities. DAN DAVIDSON

the beauty of this rugged river canyon, an opportunity which can also be enjoyed by non-anglers.

Over the centuries the river has cut down through many layers of volcanic rock, which flowed through this valley as lava when the Cascade Range was formed. The resulting erosion left colorful sheer cliffs along the river, as well as rocky outcroppings and underwater ledges that can be glimpsed on the river's bottom. The canyon is heavily timbered with big Douglas fir.

State Route 138 in southwestern Oregon parallels the river for most of its length and provides easy access from both the east and west sides of the Cascade Range. From the west, take the Roseburg City Center exit off Interstate 5 and follow the markers for Route 138 east through the little town of Glide. From the east side of the mountains, take Route 138 west from its junction with U.S. Highway 97 and

follow signs past Diamond Lake until the highway drops down into the North Umpqua canyon and finds the river. From either direction, the Steamboat Inn, about 40 miles east of Roseburg, should be one of your first stops along the North Umpqua River. Located on a bluff above some of the best fly-fishing water on the North Umpqua, the Steamboat Inn has a colorful history.

The inn traces its origins to the early 1930s, when a fishing camp was run at a site across the river by Clarence Gordon, a legendary figure on the North Umpqua. In the early 1950s, the Forest Service moved Gordon and his camp across the river to its present site to make room for a new ranger station. The site the inn now occupies was once a camping spot for Zane Grey and friends, who had moved north from the Rogue to fish the North Umpqua in the mid-1930s, because Grey believed the Rogue had

become too crowded. He found the fishing on the North Umpqua so much to his liking that he wrote only one article about it, fearing that too much publicity would ruin a good thing. In his new location, Clarence Gordon constructed the Steamboat Inn's main dining room, with its massive stone fireplace and the long community table, hewn from a single sugar pine tree. Over the years, the river gained a national reputation as a place where anglers could battle big summer steelhead in a pristine setting, and the Steamboat Inn acquired fame as a place to meet fellow fishermen and the colorful characters who lived along the river. In 1966, the camaraderie was formalized with the launching of the Steamboaters, a group formed to protect the river and to promote fly fishing.

Today the Steamboat Inn still plays host to an international cast of anglers, who come to test themselves

Above: The Fisherman's Dinner at the Steamboat Inn is served one half-hour after sunset in summer, to allow anglers their last, best chance at a steelhead.
Left: The Steamboat Inn has gained a reputation as a meeting place for both fly anglers and country-inn fanciers.
Left top: The Steamboat Inn on the North Umpqua River traces its origins to the old fishing camps of the 1930s. Zane Grey, the famed Westerns author, made his camp on the present site of the Inn.
CHARLIE BORLAND PHOTOS

47

against the swift river and its magnificent fish. When Jim and Sharon Van Loan purchased the Steamboat Inn in 1975, another social current was beginning to wash a brand new group of sophisticated, urbane travelers upriver to savor the inn's pleasures.

Country inns, always popular with visitors to Europe and Japan, offer high-quality lodging places beyond the formica tabletops and sterile sameness of motels along the nation's interstate highways. Because the Steamboat Inn features both a spectacular setting and a gourmet-quality evening meal, it has been included in all the major guides to country inns on the West Coast.

Meals always have been hearty at the Steamboat Inn, to satisfy hungry fishermen after a long day on the river. But in recent years, Sharon Van Loan and inn manager Pat Lee, who doubles as one of the most able of patient fishing guides along the river, have distilled a decade of culinary collaboration into the event known as the Fisherman's Dinner. Legend has it that Clarence Gordon's cooks at the old fishing camps insisted on serving dinner promptly at 7 p.m., despite the fact that the best fishing of the day—in the fading evening light—often occurred at just about that time or even later on long summer days. The cooks earned the undying enmity of the fishermen, who were forced to choose between eating and fishing! So, in deference to the angling art, today the big evening meal at the Steamboat Inn begins 30 minutes after sunset, to allow die-hard anglers their last, best chance at hooking a summer steelhead.

The Fisherman's Dinner begins with hors d'oeuvres and wine, served on the glassed-in back porch of the inn, where guests are encouraged to meet and mingle. The meal itself, which usually consists of four or five courses, more wine, and a no-holds-barred dessert, is served family-style at the long sugar pine table of the main dining room.

Meals at the Steamboat Inn fit in with what many chefs recognize as an emerging new Northwest cuisine. The emphasis is on the freshest possible ingredients— seasonal seafood and local lamb and beef, as well as garden-fresh vegetables and herbs. The preparation style is quick and light, befitting today's trends away from heavy, calorie-laden sauces and entrees.

Sharon and Pat manage the bustling kitchen, but Jim sometimes contributes one of his specialties at the barbecue, perhaps grilled salmon or beef tenderloin. "We try hard to pamper our guests," says Sharon Van Loan, "and they seem to keep coming back year after year, so we must be doing it right."

In response to increased summer demand, the Steamboat Inn recently complemented its original eight cabins along the river with a cluster of new cottages on a bench along Steamboat Creek. Even so, travelers find that summer bookings are difficult to obtain without an advance reservation. Of course, there's much more to do along the North Umpqua than just fish for steelhead and eat at the Steamboat Inn. The Forest Service maintains several good campgrounds along the river and the area is blessed with many fine hiking trails, suitable for everything from an easy afternoon stroll to a multi-day backpacking trip. Of special interest is the Mott Trail, which runs along the south side of the North Umpqua, opposite the road. It's a wide, well maintained path that gives hikers a view of how anglers traveled along the North Umpqua before the highway was built.

You can get an even closer view of the river in an inflatable raft. The North Umpqua's rapids are closely spaced, with plenty of rocks to negotiate, and the water is usually ice-cold in spring and early summer, the only time when there's enough water in the river for safe rafting.

There are no huge rapids on the North Umpqua, but the river demands constant respect. One of the most challenging rapids is called Pinball—it would be an apt name for almost any stretch of white water on this river—because there's virtually no way to run the rapid in a raft without bouncing off at least one or two rocks.

The first time through, it's a good idea to go with an experienced guide. A guide can also show you how to avoid disturbing fly fishermen, who tend to get very upset if you scare away the summer steelhead they've been stalking for the last half hour. On my most recent raft trip on the North Umpqua, our guide, Beth Steinberg of Ouzel Outfitters, prepared a delectable evening meal in camp that featured *coq au vin,* wild rice and chocolate fondue for dessert. In addition, we were treated to a tasting of Oregon wines from Hinman Vineyards in Eugene.

Although summer and fall are the most popular seasons along the river—the fall colors can be spectacular in the canyon—many seasoned visitors cherish the winter season. It's easier to reserve a cabin at the Steamboat Inn in the winter and, even though the big Fisherman's Dinner isn't served every night in the off-season, Pat and Sharon

Above: *A frothing falls presents a formidable barrier to salmon and steelhead as they ascend the North Umpqua.* BOB HARVEY
Facing page: *Clearwater Creek, in the headwaters of the North Umpqua River, runs through thick stands of Douglas fir trees.* CHARLIE BORLAND

always prepare a nice dinner for every guest. They might even serve it to you in your cabin, if you ask them nicely.

Excellent cross-country skiing can be found less than an hour's drive away, in the Diamond Lake area. Winter also can be an ideal time to use the Steamboat Inn as an escape hatch. Just curl up with a good book, listen to the rain drumming on the cabin roof, and watch the river.

Before you leave the Umpqua Valley, be sure to sample some of its other attractions. There are five wineries in the Roseburg area where sampling is definitely the order of the day. Hillcrest Vineyards, west of Roseburg, is the oldest winery producing fine wines in the state. Richard Sommer's bottlings are made from riesling, cabernet sauvignon, pinot noir and other grape varieties. Nearby is the Garden Valley Vineyards, where you can sample an excellent German-style gewurztraminer and other wines. A few miles to the north is the Henry Winery, whose chardonnay, gewurztraminer and pinot noir varieties are well known.

Girardet Wine Cellars, known for its prize-winning riesling wines, is a few miles south of Roseburg, near the little town of Tenmile. Take the Winston exit off Interstate 5 south of Roseburg to find Girardet and you will also be near Jonicole Vineyards, which dedicates itself to the production of cabernet sauvignon, pinot noir, gewurztraminer and chardonnay wines.

Near Jonicole Vineyards is the entrance to Wildlife Safari. Even though I've never been a great fan of zoos, I've enjoyed my visits to Wildlife Safari immensely. It's built on the model of most new wildlife parks: the visitors ride around in cages (their cars!) and the animals roam freely across the extensive grounds.

The terrain here even looks like the savannah lands of Africa, with open grassland and groves of brushy trees. Ostriches, gazelles, rhinoceroses and elephants patrol the open compound. There are exotic animals from locales on almost every continent. One of the highlights at Wildlife Safari is the big-cat compound, where tigers, leopards and the largest U.S. collection of rare cheetahs can be found.

Laurie Marker, who's worked at Wildlife Safari for over a decade, has been instrumental in developing an internationally-known cheetah breeding program at the park. She has raised several cheetahs by hand, including

Above: *Cheetahs, an endangered species in their native Africa, have been successfully bred and raised at Wildlife Safari, near Winston.*
Left: *At Wildlife Safari, exotic animals from almost every continent roam the hillsides while visitors tour the grounds in the safety of their vehicles.* MARK HOY PHOTOS

Facing page: *Paddle rafters prepare to negotiate a steep rapids on the North Umpqua. Rafting outfitters offer overnight trips on this scenic, boulder-strewn river during spring run-off.* JOHN DAUGIRDA

Khayam, a cat who starred in a TV special, on talk shows, and in hundreds of personal appearances for Wildlife Safari. Khayam died of kidney failure in 1986 and a striking bronze statue of her now stands near the entrance to Wildlife Safari.

Klamath Basin

TAKE IT EASY RANCH
KLAMATH BASIN WILDLIFE REFUGES
CRATER LAKE NATIONAL PARK

Above: *Trumpeter swan in flight.*
DAN DAVIDSON
Right: *Klamath Lake: water in abundance. And where there is water, wildlife usually can be found.*
GEORGE WUERTHNER

The Klamath basin of southwestern Oregon doesn't look anything like a bird watcher's paradise. This is open, windswept country, the beginning of the basin-and-range terrain that continues right across Eastern Oregon. It's hot here in the summer, cold in the winter. With few trees to break its force, the wind often cuts across the Klamath basin hills and valleys like a knife blade. But appearances can deceive. The Klamath country has water in abundance—and where there's water, wildlife usually can be found. The Klamath River and tributaries, along with big Klamath Lake and its marshy borders, are home to one of the largest concentrations of migrating waterfowl remaining in the United States. In winter, the largest flock of bald eagles in the lower 48 states gathers here to prey on the abundant waterfowl in the marshes.

Before white men appeared on the scene, it is estimated that more than 6 million ducks and geese migrated through the Klamath basin, taking full advantage of about 185,000 acres of shallow lakes and marshes to feed and rest. Many of these birds spent summers on their breeding grounds in Canada and Alaska, passed through the Klamath basin on their way south to wintering grounds in California, and returned north through the basin in the spring.

In 1905, the U.S. Bureau of Reclamation initiated a project to reclaim much of the marshy land in the Klamath basin and turn it into farmland. The project succeeded so well that today less than 25 percent of the original marshland remains. The reclaimed land now supports a thriving local agricultural community that harvests potatoes and various grain crops. Fortunately for the birds, early conservationists succeeded in preserving some of the original marshland for waterfowl. President Theodore Roosevelt established the nation's first waterfowl refuge, Lower Klamath National Wildlife Refuge, here in 1908. Other areas have been added to the Klamath Basin Wildlife Refuges over the years and today there are six separate units, each with its own distinctive terrain and set of bird habitats. It's estimated that more than a million birds pass through the area on their yearly migrations.

The Lower Klamath Wildlife Refuge straddles the border between Oregon and California, a few miles south of the town of Klamath Falls. If you are passing through on

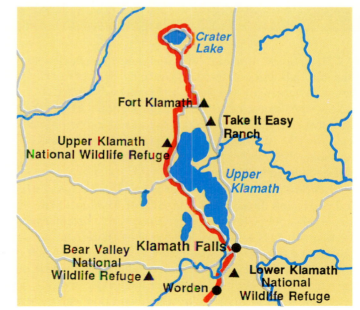

Above: *The Klamath Basin is a major stop-over area on the West Coast flyway for many migratory bird species. The area supports one of the largest concentrations of migrating waterfowl, such as these Canada geese, remaining in the United States.* DAN DAVIDSON

Above: The Lower Klamath National Wildlife Refuge was established by President Theodore Roosevelt in 1908. More than a million birds pass through on their yearly migrations.
CHARLIE BORLAND

Right: The Bear Valley Wildlife Refuge was designated to protect a roosting area for several hundred bald eagles, who gather here in winter to prey on sick or injured waterfowl in the marshes.
DAN DAVIDSON

U.S. Highway 97, turn east on State Route 161, which will take you right through the diked, marshy areas of the refuge, where many species of birds can be observed. Follow signs along the road to refuge headquarters. There the excellent visitor center has displays and information on waterfowl, as well as maps and directions for self-guided auto tours through the Lower Klamath and Tule Lake units of the refuge in California.

Returning toward Klamath Falls via U.S. Highway 97, and you'll pass through the little town of Worden. On a January morning a few years ago, I met with a group from the Klamath Falls Audubon Society. They guided me along a maze of dirt roads to a spot where we all grudgingly left the comfort of our cars and huddled together by the side of the road, trying to stay warm. Just as the first light was beginning to show in the eastern sky, someone with

especially sharp eyesight called out and pointed excitedly to a spot above the northern horizon.

As we peered through our binoculars, we saw a lone bald eagle get larger and larger in our viewframes, then wing placidly over our heads on powerful strokes. It was followed by another and then another. Then so many bald eagles began to soar over us, in twos and threes, that even dedicated birders couldn't keep track of their numbers.

This was the "morning fly out" of bald eagles from the refuge in Bear Valley, one of the roosting areas that hold 300 to 500 eagles each winter. At dawn, the eagles fly from their evening roosts—an area that's now closed to human entry through the winter months to prevent disturbance—to the Lower Klamath and Tule Lake refuges, where they hunt for sick or injured ducks and geese. If you're the type of person who can rise and shine before dawn for a wildlife spectacle, the "morning fly out" is an event worth seeing.

Continue north from Worden on U.S. 97 and take the turnoff for State Route 140 west, toward Lake of the Woods. The highway follows the west edge of Klamath Lake and the views across the big lake and its surrounding marsh make this a fine scenic drive. At the junction where Route 140 turns west, away from the lake, and climbs toward Lake of the Woods, continue north on County Road 531. The marshy area on your right is part of the Upper Klamath National Wildlife Refuge. This marsh is accessible only by boat and is closed to public access from spring through fall, to protect fragile nesting areas. There is, however, a self-guided canoe trail that will take you through part of the marsh (you'll need your own canoe). The canoe trail provides good viewing opportunities for both birding and photography.

Follow County Road 531 to its junction with State Route 62 near the crossroads town of Fort Klamath, then follow Route 62 south (right turn) past the junction with State Route 232. Here you will discover one of the most interesting little resorts in Oregon. Take It Easy Ranch bills itself as a fly-fishing resort—and it's certainly close to heaven-on-earth for fly-fishing fanatics—but all you really need is an appreciation of beautiful country to enjoy yourself at Take It Easy.

Located just a few miles south of Crater Lake National Park, the ranch sits at the base of a steep rimrock ridge. Lodgepole pine and wildflowers dot the countryside. During the resort's season—late April through the end of October—the weather is uniformly warm and sunny, with only by an occasional thunderstorm to liven things up.

Take It Easy's focus is on the two spring-fed creeks that run through the property. Their water, which percolates down through the lava from snowfields around Crater Lake, is as clear and clean as the air itself.

Randy Sparacino, who came north from the San Jose area with his wife Cynthia a few years ago to operate Take It Easy Ranch, treats the two spring creeks as his own specialized form of landscape architecture. Every log and rock in the creeks has been strategically placed, designed to produce the perfect combination of feeding and hiding habitat for the big rainbow trout that glide effortlessly

Above: Take It Easy Ranch is heaven on earth for trout anglers, but anyone with an eye for natural beauty can appreciate this fertile valley in the rimrock.
Left: The two spring creeks at Take It Easy Ranch are a specialized form of landscape architecture. Every log and rock has been strategically placed to benefit the big rainbow trout. MARK HOY PHOTOS

Although the foliage is strikingly different, the ranch streams meander with the heart and soul of English chalkstreams. Like beautiful formal gardens, they exist for the eye to savor. As with fine wines, your appreciation of them increases with familiarity. In the midst of the wild Northwest, the English vision of civilized trout fishing has been reborn at Take It Easy.

The atmosphere at the ranch reflects comfortable camaraderie, rather than the avid competition you might expect from trout anglers. Total capacity is only 20 to 25 guests, and the total number of prime fishing stations and big trout far outnumber the fishermen. Cynthia's delightful cooking is devoured twice daily (breakfast and dinner) in the log-cabin-style dining room in the main lodge. Meals are served around big circular tables, which encourages the guests to pass around some tall fishing stories right along with the entrees. Wine is served with dinner. Fishermen are inclined to dress and converse casually in social situations, which seems to fit the Sparacinos' style perfectly.

To reach the 10 cabins, guests must cross a wooden bridge over one of the ranch's streams, Fort Creek. Below the bridge, in a no-fishing area, lurks a collection of genuinely huge trout that thrive on table scraps fed to them surreptitiously by the guests. After a few minutes of watching these piscine pets, any true-blue trout fisherman will be primed for the attack.

But Take It Easy isn't just for fishermen. For those calm souls who can content themselves with just watching, the stream bank in front of the cabins at Take It Easy is better than any aquarium. From this prime vantage point, you can while away an entire afternoon, as the big trout frolic in full view in their transparent playground.

Anglers and non-anglers alike will also want to visit nearby Crater Lake National Park. The long drive around Crater Lake's rim is awe-inspiring, and a trip around the same circuit on cross-country skis in winter leads you into a back-country wonderland. But since Oregon's only national park has been described at length in many tour guides and is clearly on the beaten path, I'll leave you next to the trout stream at Take It Easy Ranch, with a problematic question: When a trout fisherman dies, would he rather go to heaven or Take It Easy?

Above: A truncated meadow in *Crater Lake National Park.* © GARY BRAASCH *Facing page: Wizard Island, Crater Lake. Formed by the eruption of Mt. Mazama 6,600 years ago, the lake is Oregon's only national park.* PAT O'HARA

through the water. Trees and bushes near the streams have been trimmed unobtrusively, to open up casting room for roaming fly anglers. Randy has not only scooped silt from the streams and replaced it with gravel, he's even placed sod on top of the fallen logs and planted it with colorful wildflower combinations.

The Sunny Skies over Bend

Century Drive
Mt. Bachelor
Rock Spring Guest Ranch
The High Desert Museum
Lava Land Visitor Center

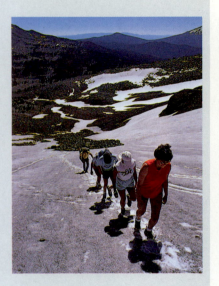

Above: *Day climbers ascending South Sister Mountain.* CHARLIE BORLAND
Right: *Bend as seen from Pilot Butte, with the Cascades in the background.* DAVE SWAN

There's a sense of excitement in the Bend area, because Central Oregon is growing and changing at a rapid pace. Like a young child who exasperates his parents by growing out of a new set of clothes almost as fast as they're fitted for him, Bend is constantly exploring new options, looking for new solutions.

The Bend area lies in a transition zone between the frosty alpine peaks of the Cascade Range and the arid, sagebrush plains that stretch away to the eastern horizon. The area's economy is also in transition, from dependence on logging and wood products-related industries to a future where tourism and high-tech industry may well become the local mainstays.

Comparisons between the Bend area and the nation's booming Sunbelt region are apt. Blessed with a sunny, dry climate, seemingly unlimited recreation potential, and a young, ambitious populace, Bend is attracting vigorous new businesses, especially young firms in computer or related high-tech fields, who are primed for growth.

But in the long run, year-round recreation probably will remain the Bend area's real specialty. One of the best ways to sample the diverse recreational resources of this region is to drive the 100-mile loop south and west of Bend known as Century Drive. From Bend, head west on the Cascade Lakes Highway (State Route 46) and follow the signs for Mt. Bachelor Ski Area. As you gain elevation and gradually climb up into the Deschutes National Forest, a grand panorama of lava flows and pine forests spreads out behind you.

When you reach the turnoff to the Mt. Bachelor Ski Area parking lot, 22 miles west of Bend, you've arrived in the heart of Oregon's winter sports mecca. Mt. Bachelor is the most popular ski area in the Northwest, annually attracting almost twice as many skiers as the next largest ski area, and it ranks in the top 15 ski areas in the U.S. One of its 11 high-speed lifts takes skiers all the way to the summit of 9,065' Mt. Bachelor, where they enjoy not only an outstanding view of surrounding peaks and wilderness areas, but also a 3,100' vertical drop to the bottom of the ski run. Mt. Bachelor also offers the most extensive network of groomed nordic ski trails in the state.

But Mt. Bachelor's success has been hard-earned. When Bill Healy arrived in Bend in the early 1950s, he

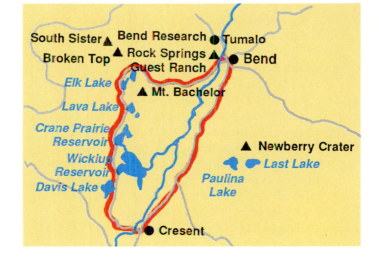

South Sister Mountain from Sparks Lake. One of the most popular recreation areas in the state, the Cascade lakes area draws outdoor enthusiasts in every season.
CHARLIE BORLAND

Sparks Lake, popular with canoeists and fly anglers, with Mt. Bachelor in the background. DAVE SWAN

found a timber town with a fantastic mountain vista, an abundance of powdery dry snow nearby, and no downhill ski area. Bill turned his hobby into a business by convincing his neighbors to invest in a fledgling ski area at Mt. Bachelor. Then he built the area from the ground up, using talented local people and his uncanny business sense.

Just as Mt. Bachelor Ski Area was beginning to hit its stride in the mid-1970s, Bill Healy was losing his ability to enjoy what he had created. First rheumatoid arthritis began cruelly to twist his hands and feet. Then Bill began to suffer balance problems, resulting in several serious skiing accidents that finally forced him to retire from the slopes.

Bill and his wife, Beverley, who had been a nurse when they first met, searched for a diagnosis and cure for Bill's health problems, but it proved elusive. Then the symptoms began to fit an ominous pattern: ALS, better known as Lou Gehrig's disease. ALS causes progressive

degeneration of the cerebral cortex and spinal column. Death usually follows within two to five years of the onset of symptoms. There is no known cure.

But Bill Healy simply refused to be served with a death warrant—he had too many plans for Mt. Bachelor. Even while all his Bend friends were honoring him with appreciative farewell dinners, Healy continued to drive himself to work every day on the mountain and develop his master plan for the ski area.

Today, Bill still directs plans for the future at Mt. Bachelor. Even though his speech is severely slurred by a loss of muscular control and he requires a walker to urge his formerly robust legs along from the car to his office, he still communicates effectively with staff and skiers alike. His expressive gray eyes convey meanings he no longer can verbalize and he continues to terrorize the locals by driving himself everywhere around Bend. And his wry smile continues to light up the face of everyone he meets. Bill Healy simply doesn't know how to quit, and that spirit has permeated Mt. Bachelor, the little ski area that could.

In winter, the snow plows clear Century Drive only as far as Mt. Bachelor, so further progress on Route 46 must be made by skis or snowmobile. Century Drive usually is cleared of snow by mid-June. If you're driving or riding your bicycle along the Century Drive loop in summer, you can ride the summit lift to the top of the mountain for a picnic and the fantastic views.

There are many other outdoor activities available along this route. It's become especially popular with cyclists in recent years, and if you ride a mountain bike, numerous gravel forest roads that connect with Century Drive expand your possibilities for exercise and exploration.

A few miles past Mt. Bachelor, a turnoff on the left leads south to Sparks Lake, a quiet fly-fishing-only lake with an abundant population of brook trout. Just opposite Sparks Lake, there's a parking area on the right (north) side of Century Drive where hikers can begin their trek up Fall Creek. A short hike up the trail takes you to a beautiful, 30′ waterfall. This is also a popular route for climbers, who hike to Green Lakes, a base for climbs up South Sister and Broken Top mountains. While these are not technically difficult climbs, they are strenuous and involve high-altitude skills. If you're a novice who would like to try climbing, inquire about a guide at one of the mountaineering equipment shops in Bend.

Century Drive takes a sharp bend to the south around Devils Lake. The next major stop is Elk Lake, a striking body of water where visitors can savor excellent views of nearby mountain peaks. The lake also offers fine fishing and strong afternoon breezes for windsurfing. The lodge at Elk Lake has a store, a grill and antique lunch counter, rustic cabins and a boat ramp. Best of all, the resort remains open in winter, when the only way to reach it is by cross-country skis or a ride in the lodge's snow-cat over 10 miles of snow-covered highway. There are many fine skiing and snowmobiling trails near Elk Lake to explore on a winter holiday at this quiet retreat.

Continuing south on Century Drive, your route will pass Lava Lake and Little Lava Lake, icy headwaters of the Deschutes River, the main river drainage through Central Oregon. There are also several access points along the west side of the road for trails leading into the nearby Three Sisters Wilderness Area, one of the most popular wilderness areas in the state. A few miles to the south, signs mark the turnoff for a paved forest road heading west to Cultus Lake. A lovely resort nestles on the shore of Cultus Lake, where good fishing, windsurfing and sailing can be enjoyed.

The next attraction along Century Drive is Crane Prairie Reservoir, considered by many fishermen to be the best fishing lake in the state. This 3,500-acre reservoir was formed in the 1930s when the Deschutes River was dammed. The river flooded a large meadow and a forest of tall pine trees, killing the trees as the water rose. The result is a collection of standing snags and fallen logjams that not only make great hiding places for the huge rainbow trout that live near them, but also provide perches for numerous osprey (fish hawks), which hunt the trout from the air.

The area around the lake is the summer home of so many osprey that it has been designated an Osprey Management Area by the Forest Service. Trails to osprey observation points along the lake begin at a designated parking area on the east side of the road. When actively feeding, the osprey put on a grand show, swooping in steep dives from their perches in the dead trees and

Above: *Elk Lake Lodge offers cabin accommodations and a rustic lunch counter. Open year-round, the lodge can be reached in winter only by snowmobile or on skis.* CHARLIE BORLAND
Left: *Bill Healy, the guiding force behind the Mt. Bachelor ski area.* DAVE SWAN

snatching fish from the water with their sharp talons. In marked contrast, the birds struggle clumsily to take off from the surface of the lake, clutching trout that are sometimes almost as large as the osprey themselves.

Crane Prairie Resort, with a camping area, store, boat rentals and a boat ramp, sits on the eastern shore of the lake. Several good Forest Service campgrounds are scattered along the lake shore.

South of Crane Prairie, Route 46 (Century Drive) intersects State Route 42. A left turn (east) here will take you over the Deschutes River at Browns Crossing on Route 42, past several other good fishing lakes and streams, to an intersection with U.S. Highway 97. But a right turn (west) at the junction of Routes 46 and 42 takes you on an unimproved road (not recommended for passenger cars) past several small alpine lakes, to the Waldo Lake Road near the big lake itself, and on to State Route 58.

If you continue south on Century Drive past this junction, your route will take you near another large reservoir, Wickiup, which has good fishing for brown and rainbow trout, as well as landlocked salmon. After passing a large lava flow on the right side of the road, you will drive near Davis Lake, a large fly-fishing-only lake that was formed several thousand years ago when this lava flow blocked Odell Creek. Davis Lake has three quiet, undeveloped campgrounds and, in addition to its good fishing for rainbow trout, supports a large and diverse population of bird life in the extensive marshes around its edge.

A few miles south of Davis Lake, Route 46 ends at a junction with County Route 61. To complete the hundred-mile loop of Century Drive, turn east and continue to the junction with U.S. Highway 97, then turn north and return to Bend.

There are several stops along U.S. 97 to be considered on your return drive, however. A few miles north of the little town of La Pine is the junction with County Route 21, a paved road that runs east and steadily uphill to Newberry Crater, a very large caldera of an old volcano, which now holds two large, scenic lakes: Paulina and East.

You'll find excellent fishing and campgrounds in the crater, as well as several good trails into the lava formations. A road to the top offers exhilarating views from this shattered mountain peak. Newberry Crater's lakes were

formed in the same manner as Crater Lake, but they don't receive the publicity (or the crowding) that goes along with national park status. The access road to Newberry Crater is closed by snow in winter, but hardy skiers and snowmobilers still manage the trip.

A few miles farther north on U.S. 97 is the access road west (left turn) to Sunriver, the site of an old military camp that has been developed into the premier all-season recreational community in Central Oregon. Located just 15 miles south of Bend, Sunriver is linked directly to the Mt. Bachelor Ski Area by a recently completed road. More than 5,000 residents live in the upscale homes and condominiums of this planned community, which features trendy shopping areas, restaurants, tennis courts, an airstrip,

frontage on the Deschutes River, and two golf courses designed by the famed Robert Trent Jones.

Continue north on U.S. 97 to the Lava Lands Visitor Center. It's located in an area of spectacular volcanism, including the large lava flow next to the visitor center and the nearby cinder cone called Lava Butte. Extensive displays and dioramas inside the center explain the volcanic history of the area, and interpretive trails allow you to explore the rugged lava flows first-hand. A road leads to the top of Lava Butte and provides a vantage point for viewing the amazing array of volcanic features nearby, including Newberry Crater and Mt. Bachelor.

A short distance north on U.S. 97, a signed access road heads east to the High Desert Museum, a privately

Above: *Native fishermen still use nets and traditional platforms to catch salmon at Sherars Falls on the lower Deschutes River.* DAVID JENSEN
Left: *An early spring outing on Century Drive near Sparks Lake.* DAVE SWAN

Facing page: *Lava Butte, a cinder cone near the Lava Lands Visitor Center, is a prime example of vulcanism in Central Oregon.* GEORGE WUERTHNER

Paulina Creek falls. STEVE TERRILL

funded center that describes the geography and culture of the high desert region through the use of innovative hands-on displays. Although it's called a museum, the emphasis here is on a working understanding of living landscapes. Much of the learning takes place along nature trails or in wildlife displays, such as the otter enclosure, where an otter family frolics in a re-created stream environment. It's highly recommended for both children and adults.

A few more minutes of driving north on U.S. 97 brings you back to the outskirts of Bend and the conclusion of the 100-mile loop. However, this is just the beginning of the recreational possibilities in and around Bend. Many other campgrounds and trails may be found in the area nearby, and the town of Bend offers surprising attractions, and a wide assortment of lodging possibilities.

For a city of fewer than 20,000 residents, Bend's menu of restaurants is diverse. Excellent French, Szechwan Chinese and Mexican restaurants, as well as many others, make your dinner choices delightfully difficult. The Pine Tavern, located on the banks of the Deschutes River next to Bend's downtown Mirror Pond park, is a traditional meeting place for locals. The restaurant building was constructed around a large pine, to avoid felling the majestic tree, whose presence has become an essential part of the dining experience at the Pine Tavern.

In appearance, Bend combines elements of a Western cow town, a New England village and a Los Angeles suburb. Handsome colonial-style frame homes dot the older residential areas near downtown Bend, where many old store fronts have been remodeled and restored in recent years. On the edge of town, growth in the last decade is apparent in the sprawling shopping malls, landscaped new housing developments and traffic snarls—another Bend surprise!

The best place to get an overview of Bend, literally, is from the top of Pilot Butte, a small volcanic cinder cone on the east edge of town. A road circles up to the top of the butte, where fine views of the city, the surrounding mountains and other volcanic features can be enjoyed.

Shopping in Bend's commercial district can be a pleasant diversion between skiing or camping trips. High-quality outdoor equipment—from skis to mountain bikes to sailboards—is available at many well stocked outdoor stores. Several galleries in downtown Bend feature fine paintings and sculpture by both locally- and nationally-known artists, with particular emphasis on wildlife and landscape subjects.

If you drive north from Bend on U.S. 97, your route will cross the Deschutes River and then bring you to the crossroads community of Tumalo. On a bluff of rimrock above Tumalo perches Bend Research, one of a growing number of high-tech companies that have located in the Bend area in recent years.

The founder of Bend Research, Harry Lonsdale, is one of the region's true visionaries. Lonsdale brought his fledgling company, which specializes in research on membrane technology, from the San Francisco Bay Area, looking for an atmosphere where he and his employees

could breathe clean air, get lots of outdoor exercise and think clearly. He's found all of that in Bend and in the interim has parlayed a $5,400 initial investment into $3.5 million in annual revenues and an impressive list of grants from government and private industry sources.

Lonsdale is a wiry, fast-talking, 55-year-old native of New Jersey who also helped establish the Oregon Innovation Network, a loosely knit group of entrepreneurs and resource people who have published a handbook to aid the growth of small businesses with big ideas. Lonsdale sees the Bend area, and other enclaves like it across Oregon and the rest of the U.S., as future havens for entrepreneurs and the growth-oriented businesses they will establish.

"Big companies don't innovate," says Lonsdale, looking out of his large plate-glass office window at an inspiring view of nearby mountain peaks. "That's something you can quote me on, underline it, and put an

Broken Top Mountain from the summit of South Sister. CHARLIE BORLAND

Inside the cinder cone at Lava Butte, near Lava Lands Visitor Center.
ANCIL NANCE

his hands through his gray hair, as if to massage his facile brain into a moment of quiet reflection.

A few miles west on Tumalo Reservoir Road from Lonsdale's Bend Research campus lies a little valley where quiet reflection and non-stop recreation go hand-in-hand. Rock Springs Guest Ranch is a dude ranch that's made the transition into the modern age as an active family resort. It offers guests an unbeatable combination: unlimited horseback riding, combined with a wide range of other outdoor activities, three hearty meals of fresh food every day, and a staff that's dedicated to making each visitor feel like a member of the Rock Springs family.

The lodge nestles at the head of a fertile, well watered valley. Riding trails meander through open ponderosa pine forests and up onto sagebrush plateaus sparsely dotted with ancient juniper trees. Fine views of the peaks in the nearby Three Sisters Wilderness Area add a satisfying Western touch.

The springs that give the ranch its name trickle down the hillside and swell into a ranch pond flanked by multi-colored boulders. Ducks and a family of Canada geese ply the waters. On the hillside above the pond perches another kind of spring, this one man-made, lined with colorful blue tiles, and set into a cave-like shelter of boulders. Here warm water bubbles up in jets over the tired bodies of ranch guests, draining away the accumulated aches and pains of a long day on the trail.

Without a doubt, this is the New West, a version of cowboy country unlike any to be found around a campfire a hundred years ago. Rock Springs Guest Ranch owes its atmosphere to Donna Gill, an independent woman with strong ideas who guided the operation through its first 13 seasons. Before she came to Rock Springs, Gill operated a summer camp for girls and then another guest ranch, which gave her the freedom to spend her off-seasons exploring the rest of the world.

In 1969, Donna returned from her annual odyssey and found the ranch of her dreams at Rock Springs. She bought it the next day. Here she built a guest ranch with families in mind. Families who, over time, turned their visits into annual vacations and became her friends as much as her customers. As the children of that first generation of guests grew up, they helped keep the traditions

exclamation point after it. Because big companies tend to be very protective—and they don't take risks."

So Bend Research has gathered 80 employees who enjoy being challenged and like to take risks. They work on projects as diverse as recycling water in NASA's planned space shuttle or development of a bio-erodible membrane to be implanted in the body for timed release of an alcohol-aversion drug.

And they don't consider themselves isolated in Central Oregon, either. On the wall behind Lonsdale's desk is a large map of the world, which he uses often to punctuate his wide-ranging visions with a quick stab of reality. Bhopal. Tokyo. Washington, D.C. Lonsdale's mind moves so quickly that he's constantly jotting down notes to himself. "I want to talk about that later," he says, rubbing

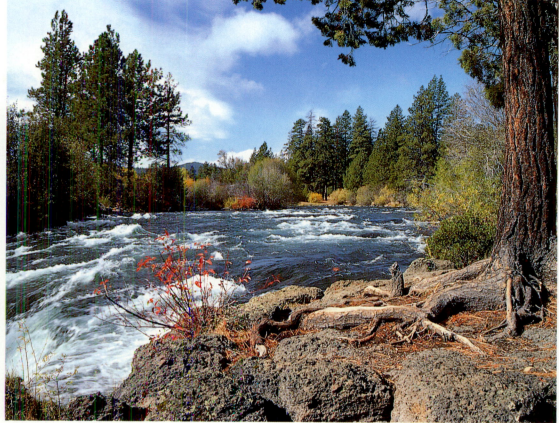

alive. Donna Gill died in 1983 but her extended family of guests continues to grow and to keep alive the atmosphere she initiated at Rock Springs.

Donna's nephew, John Gill, is a tall, soft-spoken man who now oversees operations at the ranch. Along with his operations manager, Jeff Schlapfer, he keeps the Gill penchant for quality alive in every arena, from the riding stables to the dining room. The resort's string of 55 horses is pastured on the premises year-round, to ensure that the saddle animals stay in prime condition. Wranglers constantly work with the horses and pride themselves on their ability to match each rider with the right mount. Beginning riders are grouped together for an easy-going learning experience, while more experienced riders explore the ranch's trail network in faster-paced groups.

There are also a swimming pool, tennis courts, volleyball and hayrides, so every member of the family can keep active. Youth counselors organize the younger members of the family into groups, so adults can enjoy the ranch on their own time. And the food is served up with an eye toward both high quality and bounteous quantity. The kitchen staff at Rock Springs appreciates how fresh mountain air can spark an appetite

That's a taste of the Bend area, where Old West hospitality meets the free-wheeling lifestyles of the New West. Where growth and change are the only constants. And even the people who live here aren't quite sure where Bend is headed—but they know they can't wait to get there.

Above: *Along the Deschutes River near Bend.* CHARLIE BORLAND
Left: *Trail riding at the Rock Springs Guest Ranch, founded by Donna Gill.* DAVE SWAN

Smith Rocks State Park

and

John Day Fossil Beds National Monument

Above: Cacti in bloom along the John Day River. ANCIL NANCE

Right: Bluffs of colorful rock at Smith Rocks State Park attract an elite corps of rock climbers from around the world. CHARLIE BORLAND

Facing page: The Crooked River slices silently through a deep canyon cut over the centuries around Smith Rocks. DAVID JENSEN

Smith Rocks is easy to miss. The highway sign on U.S. Highway 97 at the crossroads village of Terrebone, a little more than 20 miles north of Bend, is small. And the winding access road (keep a sharp eye out for signs directing you to the park) gives little indication that you're headed toward an international attraction.

Smith Rocks State Park attracts a very special type of visitor. The steep bluffs of colorful rock across the Crooked River loom larger, and to the elite corps of rock climbers who are drawn to them, these palisades present a challenge as imposing as any in North America.

Rock climbers are a breed apart. They're not fascinated by the idea of forming an expedition to assault Mt. Everest, or trudging up the volcanic cones in the Oregon Cascades. And while most climbers take pride in the list of towering peaks they've conquered, rock climbers take a micro approach to their sport. Their eyes gleam as they recall ascending one vertical rock face, or even just one short, but treacherously difficult, section of that face. Getting to the top isn't nearly as important to them as the style you show in the process of getting there.

In recent years, rock climbers have pioneered more than 280 routes up the colorful bluffs at Smith Rocks. They've given the routes some exotic names, such as Crack of Infinity, the Young and the Restless, I Almost Died, Calamity Jam and Deteriorata—names that reflect their eccentric sense of humor and the role of the true individualist in their sport. Now that climbing magazines have begun to describe these routes as the most challenging collection of "free climbs" in North America, the routes at Smith Rocks are on the lips of even the most elite climbers from Europe.

If you had chanced upon Smith Rocks State Park, expecting a pleasant picnic site, you might have been excused for wondering why the people in the primitive campsite near the picnic grounds seemed to be speaking in a babel of foreign tongues. Or why they're dressed in skin-tight outfits of the most amazing patterns and Day-Glo colors. But now you can nod your head knowingly and mosey down the path to the observation point to watch the best rock climbers in the world do their thing.

Rock climbing isn't really a spectator sport. There are no programs or announcers to comment on particularly

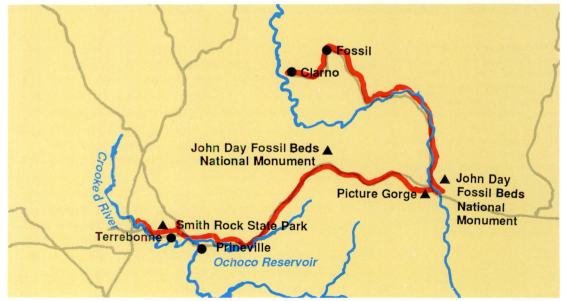

awesome moves by the participants. But a few minutes spent watching these people as they flit up vertical rock faces with no visible means of support, will convince you that these are among the finest athletes anywhere. They look a bit like colorful bugs (binoculars are a big help here) as you watch them from the observation point across the river, so try descending the trail, crossing the bridge over the Crooked River and walking the path that follows along the base of the rocks.

You'll discover that Smith Rocks has a stark beauty all its own, with hawks swooping along the steep rock faces and the Crooked River slicing silently through the deep canyon it cut over the centuries. Hollywood movie directors think so, too. Scenes for several movies, including *Rooster Cogburn* with John Wayne, have been shot here, as well as a few TV commercials.

If you enjoy roughing it, you may want to stay overnight at the bivouac campground used by the climbers. There are no facilities for recreational vehicles here, although there is a rustic store at nearby Juniper Junction. You will probably find that climbers are an eccentric, intriguing lot. And you will certainly be able to tell your friends some first-class stories about this bohemian enclave in the wilds of Central Oregon.

Instead of retracing your route to U.S. 97, follow the signs pointing east toward Prineville, on a series of back roads along the valley of the Crooked River. This country is blessed with irrigation water from the river, so it's lush and green. Keep a sharp eye out for songbirds, waterfowl and hawks on the wing.

In Prineville, turn east on the main street through town (U.S. Highway 26) and head for the John Day

country. The route will take you past Ochoco Lake, where there's fine fishing, and up into the Ochoco National Forest. With the elevation gain, the stands of ponderosa pine and larch trees get thicker and more impressive. This scenic drive takes you all the way up to a 4,720′ summit, but before reaching the top you'll probably want to stop and explore one of the roadside meadows crisscrossed by winding trout streams. Or perhaps sit quietly in a grove of ponderosa pines, known locally as "yellow bellies" for their massive golden trunks.

Beyond the Ochoco summit, the road descends into a completely different type of terrain, the dry, wind-blown canyon land characteristic of the John Day country. Just before you reach the little town of Mitchell, take a left (north) turn on the signed road to the Painted Hills unit of the John Day Fossil Beds National Monument. With an

Volcanic ash formations have weathered into fantastic shapes in the Blue Basin area of the John Day Fossil Beds National Monument.
DAVID JENSEN

rounded, dune-like hills resulted, in such pleasing color combinations that professional photographers make up a high percentage of the hardy souls who venture here. Several trails with informational stops along the way are maintained by the Park Service.

If a visit to the Painted Hills has whetted your curiosity about the geology of this area, your next stop should be the Cant Ranch Visitor Center. Return to U.S. 26 and follow it east to its junction with State Route 19. You are now in what's known as the Picture Gorge of the John Day River. It's an impressive gorge cut down through the lava flows by the John Day River, and is definitely worthy of further exploration. However, to reach the Visitor Center, turn left (north) on Route 19 and a few minutes of driving will bring you to Cant Ranch.

Visitor centers in national parks or monuments tend to have a sameness about them, but Cant Ranch is unique, an attraction all its own. The ranch house was built in 1917 by James Cant, a Scotchman who came to Eastern Oregon and became a sheep rancher. In one room of the house, the interior has been preserved much as it looked 60 years ago. Farm implements still are scattered around the grounds. And the bunkhouse museum tells the story of the early paleontologists who came to this remote area to collect samples.

The scientists were drawn here by the finds of Rev. Thomas Condon, a Methodist minister from Fort Dalles on the Columbia River. The father of geological study in Oregon, Condon sent samples of his finds in this area to the Smithsonian Institution in 1870. Analysis there by geologists revealed that Condon had discovered an uninterrupted fossil record that went back over 7 million years. Many world-famous paleontologists made the pilgrimage to the John Day country in the late 19th century to collect fossil samples. Later, they were joined by amateur collectors, who continued to remove pieces of the fossil record from the area until Congress finally took action to preserve the fossil beds by creating a national monument in 1974.

The staff at John Day Fossil Beds has time to explain the area's geology to visitors. As one ranger stated, almost every child goes through a period of fascination with dinosaurs, and here is a place to reawaken your fantasies. Here, those dry geology textbooks come alive.

impressive title like that, you might expect a large government outpost, but this is one of the most remote and rarely visited attractions in Oregon.

The Painted Hills were formed by ashfalls from a series of volcanic eruptions millions of years ago. The layers of ash in a range of colors, mostly buff and red hues, in alternating strata. Over the centuries, they've been weathered by the sandblasting wind, infrequent rain and flash floods that characterize this countryside. A series of

Millions of years ago, Eastern Oregon had a much wetter climate—almost tropical, according to the fossils of palm, fern and other leaves that have been found. An assortment of hoofed creatures and their predators also roamed the savannah. Periodic eruptions from volcanoes buried some areas, which then sprouted new plant life as the rock weathered into soils. Eventually, the rising line of volcanoes we know today as the Cascade Range cut off moisture from the ocean and turned the John Day country into its present arid landscape.

A few miles north of the Cant Ranch, trails lead into an area known as Blue Basin and provide us with a glimpse of the geological processes at work, as well as the sites of some famous fossil finds. This is rough, dry country, so dress appropriately. The Overlook Trail is a four-mile round-trip with a real bonus—an outstanding panorama of the John Day River canyon below.

The Clarno unit, the third unit of the John Day Fossil Beds, is reached by driving north on Route 19 to the small town of Fossil, then turning south on State Route 218. The principal features here are eroded mudslides, which exhibit a range of colors in brown and bronze.

There are no campgrounds in the John Day Fossil Beds National Monument, so obtain either a list of local campgrounds at the Cant Ranch Visitor Center or continue east on U.S. 26 to the towns of Mt. Vernon or John Day, where motels and restaurants are available.

Above: *An uninterrupted fossil record spanning 7 million years drew scientists from all over the world to the fossil beds in Central Oregon.*
Left: *Layers of volcanic ash in a range of pleasing colors form the rounded hillsides of the Painted Hills, a unit of the John Day Fossil Beds National Monument.*
DAVID JENSEN PHOTOS

Southeast Oregon

Above: CHARLIE BORLAND
Right: *A gravel road winds through Leslie Gulch in southeastern Oregon, a land where surprises can be expected.* DAVID JENSEN

When I look at a map of Oregon, the southeastern quadrant of the state reminds me of an old explorers' map, the kind that had large empty sections filled only with the notation "unexplored territory."

To most people, southeastern Oregon is unexplored territory—a vast wasteland. And the prospect of so much wide-open country is intimidating, if not downright scary. In this part of the state it's easy to drive a hundred miles and never see a gas station. And motels—well, you know you've landed in one of the major outposts of civilization in this part of the world if it boasts a motel.

For someone who craves wide-open spaces, all that "unexplored territory" is a just cause for celebration. To me, it means I can come back year after year and still discover country I haven't seen, people I haven't met, and maybe even find stories that still need to be told.

People really do live in southeastern Oregon—there's just a lot more space between them out here. This is arid country and no one has figured out yet how to make this part of the high desert bloom. So people here usually live either on sprawling cattle ranches or in tiny crossroads communities, where they still gather at the local cafe to exchange news over a cup of coffee.

Southeastern Oregon is high desert country, but that doesn't mean it's all flat land to the horizon. Far from it. There are mountain ranges here that were scraped clean by the glaciers formed on their slopes during the last ice age. And there are huge alkaline lakes with no outlet to the sea, many shrunken now to only a fraction of their former size. In between the mountains and the alkaline lakes are deeply carved canyons that hold wildlife, quaking aspen trees, and, sometimes, steaming pools of hot springs, bubbling up to the surface. Like the "unexplored territory" on the adventurers' maps, this is country where you expect surprises. They're the reason you come here.

But first a few words of caution. If you don't want to subject your car to dusty, pothole-filled dirt roads, your exploration of southeastern Oregon will be severely limited, to just a handful of the places I'll mention below. And even if you do limit your travels to paved roads, it's a good idea to carry spare water and fuel along with you, as well as a good spare tire (preferably two). A four-wheel-drive vehicle is nice; an old, indestructible pickup truck is even better.

Be prepared to pull over and sleep in the car or pitch your tent in open country. Campgrounds are few and far between. On the plus side, it rains so infrequently in the high desert that you can often simply roll out your sleeping bag under the stars—a real treat when there are, as one famous astronomer put it, "billions and billions" of stars to watch as you drift off to sleep.

The only logical place to resupply your food and gasoline stocks in southeastern Oregon is the town of Burns. For this part of the world, it's a veritable urban beehive, with several big supermarkets, gas stations and auto repair shops, motels and restaurants. Burns is also the intersection point of the three main highways that provide access to southeastern Oregon. U.S. Highway 20, which runs east-west from Ontario to Bend through Burns, is the most heavily traveled route through the region. U.S. Highway 395 runs north-south from the John Day country

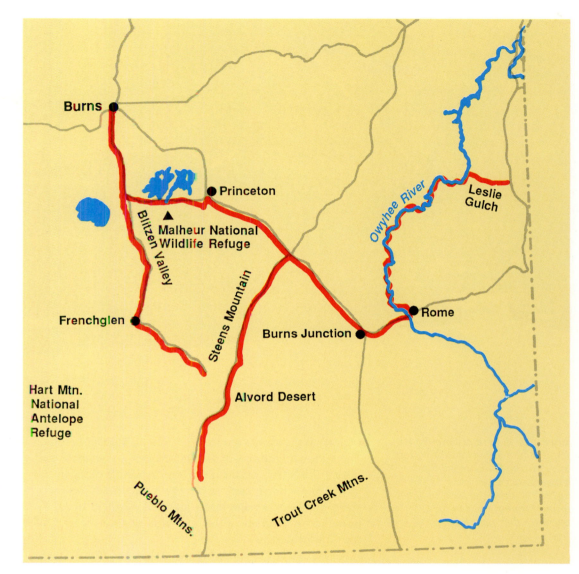

through Burns to Lakeview in the south. State Route 78 heads southeast from Burns to intersect with U.S. Highway 95, which cuts across a corner of Oregon between Idaho and Nevada.

Many travelers who visit southeastern Oregon, as opposed to those who are just passing through at high speed on one of the main highways, come to see the

Above: The store in historic French-glen is a gathering place for visitors to the nearby Malheur Wildlife Refuge. GEORGE WUERTHNER
Right: The steaming pools of a hot springs form an oasis in the sagebrush flats near the Alvord Desert. DIANE KELSAY

region's best-known attraction, Malheur Wildlife Refuge. The spring migrations of sandhill cranes, snow geese and other birds attract enthusiasts from hundreds of miles away. And while it can't match the Klamath refuges for sheer numbers of migrating waterfowl, Malheur boasts tremendous diversity of wading birds, songbirds, birds of prey and waterfowl.

To reach the wildlife refuge, take State Route 78 east from Burns. After a very short distance, turn south on State Route 205 and follow signs to the refuge. The highway climbs steeply up an old lava cap that has stubbornly resisted erosion. At the top, pull over at the viewpoint and take some time to look down at the vastness of Malheur Lake, currently the largest lake in the Northwest.

I say "currently" because Malheur Lake rests in a broad sink which catches the melted snow run-off from Steens Mountain, usually visible on the southern horizon,

and the Strawberry Mountains to the north. In dry years, Malheur Lake has been known to go completely dry. In wet years, which have been predominant recently, the lake fills up, merges with nearby Harney Lake and spreads out across the sagebrush flats. In its most recent wet phase, Malheur Lake drowned several ranches, as well as a railroad line and quite a few miles of highway roadbed.

In fact, as you follow Route 205 down off your high vantage point and across the lake, notice that the roadbed you're riding on has been elevated several feet to keep it above water. Malheur means misfortune or unhappiness in French and, true to its name, the rising lake water has caused tremendous dislocation not only to the human population of the area, but to the refuge's wildlife as well. Most of the prime nesting areas for waterfowl in the lake's marshy borders have been flooded and the sage uplands now at the lake's edge do not provide the necessary cover for nesting birds. However, since the lake level shows no sign of a fast retreat in the near future, both humans and wildlife are learning to adapt.

Just beyond the southern edge of Malheur Lake, turn east on a paved road and follow signs that direct you to the refuge headquarters. This road formerly paralleled the lake shore, but its low-lying sections now are flooded, so a detour takes you past the Malheur Field Station.

The field station is a collection of World War II–vintage barracks buildings, sandwiched between two low buttes. It's maintained by a consortium of Northwest colleges as a residential school where students can study desert ecology and wildlife. The field station is also a favorite gathering place for conferences of birders and conservationists, who regard its isolation and access to prime birding areas as a bonus.

Since public accommodations are nonexistent in this area, you can arrange to stay in the field station's spartan dormitory housing, if you call ahead. (If no other groups are on-site, you may have to bring and cook your own food, however.) While the field station lacks amenities, its prime location is more than adequate compensation.

If you continue past the field station on the gravel road and follow signs, you will discover the refuge head-quarters in a grove of cottonwood trees, where it formerly commanded a fine view of a marshy waterfowl breeding area. It now looks out over the oceanic expanse of Malheur Lake. Inside, you can find maps for the self-guided auto tour of the refuge. Just down the hill is an amazing little museum building, where more than 250 exquisite specimens of birds can be viewed.

Malheur Wildlife Refuge covers 183,000 acres and may well be the best place in Oregon to view wildlife. But unlike other areas where I've suggested that hiking is the best way to really see an area, the main refuge at Malheur is simply too large to cover on foot. In fact, it would take several days just to explore all the access roads at Malheur. The best solution is to use your car as a blind—that is, cruise slowly along the dike roads described in the auto tour until you spot wildlife, then turn off your motor and use your binoculars or a telephoto lens to zero in. More than 280 species of birds and more than 55 species of mammals have been recorded on the refuge.

Above: Picturesque Strawberry Lake captures its cold, clear water from snowmelt off the Strawberry Mountains, north of Malheur Lake. GEORGE WUERTHNER

Left: American white pelicans and great blue herons are among the scores of birds and animals that can be observed at Malheur Wildlife Refuge. © GARY BRAASCH

At the southern end of the Blitzen Valley, which is primarily refuge land, lies the little crossroads town of Frenchglen. Meals and lodging are available here at the Frenchglen Hotel, a small, restored stagecoach stop that is operated by the State of Oregon as a historic wayside. The hotel has eight small bedrooms and serves a home-style evening meal, but you'll need to make reservations in advance. Nearby, the Bureau of Land Management operates a campground in a lush little canyon at Page Springs.

The whole Blitzen Valley is filled with marshy lowlands that are home to many birds and animals. A series of lava formations at nearby Diamond Craters also begs for exploration. In this smaller section of the Malheur Refuge it's more appropriate to explore on foot, following a section of what's known as the Desert Trail. One trail section runs from Page Springs campground to Diamond Craters, passing through marshy lowland areas that are prime birding spots, and upland sage flats, where deer and antelope often can be viewed.

A few years ago, I had the privilege of hiking part of this trail with Russ Pengelly, the genial, soft-spoken man who has championed the idea of a Desert Trail for many years. We sat on a windy bluff overlooking Krumbo Reservoir as Russ talked about the great treasures and resources that are to be found in desert lands. Russ firmly believes that the best way to introduce people to the beauty of the desert is by hiking.

With a few precautions, such as knowledge about water purification and how to avoid snake problems, the desert hiker can get in touch with the landscape on an intimate basis. Geology, vegetation zones and water conservation all become real-life issues as you wind through the canyons and open basins along the trail. In many places, there is no set trail of the type we're accustomed to seeing in alpine hiking; instead, a corridor is defined from one point to the next and the hiker chooses his or her own path through rocks or sagebrush to get to the destination.

Russ shares a grand dream with fellow hikers in several Western states. They dream of a National Scenic Desert Trail, stretching from the Mexican border all the way to Canada, through arid lands. Several sections of the trail already have been mapped in southeastern Oregon

(maps available from the Desert Trail Association in Burns). Eventually, Russ hopes these trail sections will be coupled with others, some of which already exist in Nevada and California. Listening to Russ talk about his dream on that windy bluff, I had the feeling that his desert trail will become a reality in just the same way the arid lands were formed—with slow, inexorable progress.

After you've seen the Blitzen Valley on a close-up-and-personal basis, return to Page Springs campground and take the Steens Mountain Loop Road for an overview of southeastern Oregon. This road usually is closed by snow until late May (some sections may remain closed until July), but when it's accessible, it provides a panoramic ride to the 9,773' summit. Steens Mountain—often called simply "the Steens" by locals—is actually a 30-mile-long range, one of several fault-block mountain ranges in southeastern Oregon. They formed when cooling lava flows cracked along fault lines and one edge of the fault dropped, while the other edge was thrust upwards, tilting giant blocks of lava into mountain ranges.

As you drive the road to the summit of the Steens, you are progressing up the gentle, tilting slope toward the fault line. At the top, the scarp falls away precipitously to the east, ending one vertical mile below on the surface of the Alvord Desert, a low, salt playa desert. During the recent wet cycle, the Alvord Desert once again has become a salty lake.

On a clear day, the summit of the Steens provides an excellent vantage point from which to survey your options for exploring southeastern Oregon. On the hazy western horizon lies another fault block range called Hart Mountain. Reached only by gravel or dirt roads that range in

Above: Due to the dedicated efforts of wildlife managers, bighorn sheep once again roam the craggy heights of fault block mountain ranges in Southeastern Oregon. GEORGE WUERTHNER

Left: The low salt playa of the Alvord Desert becomes a shallow lake during wet cycles. CHARLIE BORLAND

Facing page: Succor Creek Canyon in the Owyhee Uplands. Deeply carved canyons invite exploration by desert hikers. DAVID JENSEN

Above: Rafters float through the serene canyons of the upper Owyhee River.
Right: The Owyhee River can be navigated only during high snow-melt years, but rapids such as the Widowmaker make it "experts only" on the upper river.
CHARLIE BORLAND PHOTOS

quality from rough to treacherous, Hart Mountain is a designated wildlife refuge for a free-roaming herd of antelope. Bighorn sheep also graze its highest craggy slopes. Below, near the refuge headquarters, is a sheltered campground with a hot-springs bath. Using the camp-ground as a base, you can hike up the mountain or down into rimrock canyons, where ancient petrogylphs can be seen on the rock walls.

South of the Steens lie two remote ranges, the Pueblo Mountains and the Trout Creek Mountains. A 22-mile section of the Desert Trail runs through the Pueblos, providing access to groves of aspen and mountain mahog-any trees along the perennial streams that water them. The Trout Creek Mountains are among the least-visited places in the state. The area is dissected by large canyons cut by Trout Creek and its tributaries, where remnant populations of the rare redband trout—specially adapted to life in arid regions—can be found.

After it emerges from the Pueblo Mountains, the Desert Trail follows a 25-mile corridor along the edge of the Alvord Desert at the base of the Steens. The Alvord Desert sizzles in summer, so this stretch of trail usually is hiked in the spring or fall. If your timing is right, a spring hike may take you through a showy wildflower display. At times, lupine blooms so heavily here that the base of the mountains looks like a solid purple band above the stark white surface of the salt playa below.

To the east, across the Alvord Desert, lie the Owyhee Uplands, a rugged section of low mountains and year-round streams that extends across the border into Idaho and south into Nevada. In the main, this open high desert region is little visited, but the Owyhee River has developed a fine reputation among rafters from all over the West Coast. To reach the Owyhee River, you should back-track to the Malheur Refuge Headquarters and proceed east on the gravel road leaving the refuge. At the intersection with

State Route 78 near the crossroads village of Princeton, turn east and drive toward Burns Junction. There are no services of any kind for the next 65 miles, so check your gas tank before leaving Princeton.

Along the way you will pass a junction where signs point south towards the Alvord Desert and the little town of Fields. This gravel road runs along the base of the Steens Mountains and is an excellent side trip for the adventurous desert traveler. Several small lakes along the route offer fishing for Lahontan trout, a variety of cutthroat trout adapted to desert conditions. There also are several hot springs along the way, including one on the Alvord Ranch (private property, but public use of the spring is allowed) where you can look out over the salt playa as you soak your dusty bones.

Back on Route 78 heading east, when you reach the junction with U.S. Highway 95 at Burns Junction, continue east (bear left) to the little town of Rome. Most rafters begin their trip at a put-in just across the bridge on the east side of the Owyhee River. The upper forks of this river also can be navigated by rafts, but it's expert water only. The rapids are formidable and it's a long walk out over the desert if you destroy your equipment.

River trips here are completely dependent on spring run-off from the surrounding mountains. In some years, when the snowpack is low or nonexistent, there isn't enough water to float a decent-sized raft. Even when there's enough water, the rocks in the Owyhee present a hazard. They're sharp—many have fallen from the canyon walls only recently—and they easily can slash a raft.

But there's something irresistible about a desert river like the Owyhee. Gliding along through canyons cut down through the lava flows over millions of years, you seem to gather in some of the land's serenity and power. You can hike up Lambert Rocks, where a series of lava flows and ash falls have formed weathered crags resembling a chocolate-and-vanilla layer cake. Or you can visit an old cabin where a rustler is said to have secreted away his stolen horses in corrals bounded by rock fences, piled up laboriously by hand.

Days on the Owyhee alternate between easy drifts through the spectacular canyon scenery and short, intense rapids, where the prospect of all those sharp rocks loom-

The open spaces of Southeastern Oregon are made to order for explorers. CHARLIE BORLAND

ing ahead brings home how truly isolated you are in this desert corner of the state. At night, you pitch your camp on a sandy beach and if you choose the right campsite, you may be able to take a long soak in a hot spring after dinner.

Our group rafted from Rome all the way downstream to Lake Owyhee, a man-made reservoir that supplies irrigation water to farmers in this lonely part of the state. There we were met by a power boat that towed our rafts to a take-out on the edge of the reservoir. After deflating the rafts and packing all our gear away, we were treated to one final surprise. As we drove on a gravel road back to U.S. 95, we passed through Leslie Gulch, a canyon where multicolored lava flows have been weathered into a variety of fantastic shapes. Driving through this valley of weird pinnacles and rainbow colors seemed a fitting end to our adventure in southeastern Oregon, where surprises are definitely the order of the day.

Wild
Wallowas

**WALLOWA MOUNTAINS
HELLS CANYON
EAGLES CAP WILDERNESS**

Above: Aster fleabane wildflowers in
the Wallowa Mountains.
© GARY BRAASCH

Right: The winter splendor of Chief
Joseph Mountain seen across the
frozen surface of Wallowa Lake.
DAVID JENSEN

On the face of it, Oregon seems like an unlikely setting for cowboys. When you think of cattle ranches, ten-gallon hats and bucking broncs, it's probably Texas or Arizona—or perhaps Montana—that comes to mind.

But there's no getting around it, northeastern Oregon is cowboy country. The region has everything you need for a romantic western novel: a history of Indian wars, periodic wild gold rushes, and big, working ranches in wide open country—with an appropriate backdrop of snow-covered mountains, of course!

If this wild west image conflicts with your ideas about Oregon—it's supposed to be rainy and they grow big fir trees there, don't they?—then join the crowd. Even the majority of Oregonians, who live in the wet Willamette Valley, know almost nothing about the four big counties that make up northeastern Oregon. Even if they've driven through this part of the state on their way to parts east, most people see little but wide open spaces—and some historic markers—along the highway. The markers commemorate the route of the Old Oregon Trail, which Interstate 84 roughly follows. The immigrant wagon trains crossed the Snake River and entered what would later become the state of Oregon near Farewell Bend, where there's now a big state park offering fishing, boating and swimming, in addition to camping.

After they lumbered across the big valley that today holds the towns of Baker and La Grande, the pioneers embarked on one of the most difficult legs of their journey west. Even today, as you zoom up the long grade into the Blue Mountains on the interstate highway, you can imagine the wear and tear that this climb must have exacted on the people, animals and wagons in those immigrant parties—especially after the rigors they had already survived.

But the pioneer wagon trains passed right by another route, this one leading to perhaps Oregon's most beautiful hidden valley—a place that many of the immigrants would probably have been happy to adopt as their new home, forsaking the uncertainties of the trail ahead. If you're a savvy traveler, you won't make the same mistake. When you reach the picturesque town of La Grande, turn northeast on State Route 82 and follow the Grande Ronde river toward the Wallowa Valley.

You'll first pass through the little towns of Imbler and Elgin, gradually working your way up to the summit of Minam Hill. Just a little more than a hundred years ago, a line of stakes marked this summit. And those stakes were

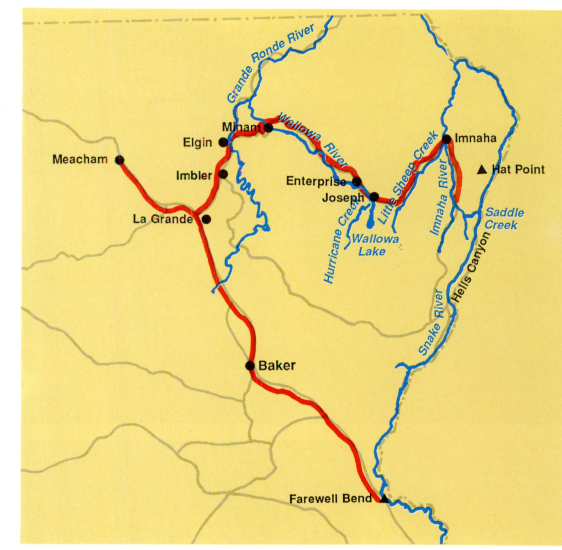

the reason the immigrants passed this valley by for so many years.

The stakes were placed there by Old Chief Joseph, head man of the Nez Perce Indians. They signaled that the entire Wallowa Valley had been ceded to his tribe as a reservation in a treaty with the U.S. Government. The valley was the traditional summer home of the Nez Perce, who hoped the natural barriers of mountain ranges and rugged canyon country that isolate the Wallowa Valley would keep the tide of white settlers away.

In many ways, the Nez Perce personified the romantic image of the "noble red man" that the first Western writers were fond of embellishing. Like the plains tribes, the Nez Perce were tall, skilled horsemen who could out-ride any competitor on the pinto ponies they bred. They lived well on the bountiful fish runs in the Snake River and the herds of deer and elk that roamed the canyon lands. The women wove intricate baskets and used elk hides for tanned clothing, which they embellished with exquisite bead work. The men were fierce warriors, but were careful not to pick fights with the whites, whom they recognized as a powerful and numerous enemy.

Unfortunately, Old Chief Joseph's stakes couldn't stem the tide of immigrants forever. The first white settlers entered the Wallowa Valley illegally and the treaty was later repudiated. After old Chief Joseph died, Young Chief Joseph continued to counsel peace. But when the authorities tried to relocate the Nez Perce to a reservation in Idaho in 1877, he and his warriors led their people on a 1,700-mile retreat—a running battle, really—that ended with their capture just 50 miles short of freedom in Canada.

When you enter the Wallowa Valley, you will immediately understand why the Nez Perce fought so hard to stay here. A green oasis in a sea of dry canyon uplands, the Wallowa Valley is watered by rivers draining high snowfields in the Wallowa Mountains to the south. On the east side of the valley is the formidable barrier of the Hells Canyon country. Cut off on all sides by natural barriers, the residents of this valley have always had to be self-sufficient, but they've also had an impressive array of natural resources on which to sustain themselves.

Gold attracted the first big wave of settlers to the region—and the economy has operated on a boom and bust basis ever since. Even though the traditional cattle and sheep ranches have suffered hard times in recent years, they still form one of the mainstays of the county's economy, along with farms that grow wheat and other grain crops. Logging in the alpine forests is still important to the local economy, too. Enterprise, the county seat, is the largest of the small towns in the Wallowa Valley. Nearby, the little town of Joseph sits at the outlet of scenic Wallowa Lake and at the base of the Wallowa Mountains. All the small towns are commercial centers for the farms and ranches scattered around the valley. But more and more, Wallowa County residents are pegging their economic future on outsiders, who come to marvel at this valley of natural wonders.

Above: *The Wallowa Valley is a green oasis, watered by rivers draining the high snowfields of the Wallowa Mountains.*
Right: *Prickly pear cactus thrives on basalt columns in the arid bottoms of Hells Canyon.* DAVID JENSEN PHOTOS

Ken Wick is an outfitter who packages trips into nearby wilderness areas, using his pack string of horses and mules to transport deer and elk hunters, fishermen and, in recent years, an increasing number of people who simply enjoy the outdoors and come to see the sights.

A couple of years ago, I rode with one of Ken Wick's pack strings as we explored the deepest gorge in North America, Hells Canyon. We drove east on State Route 350 from his ranch near Joseph to the canyonland town of Imnaha. From Imnaha, you can drive east on a rough road (not recommended for passenger cars in wet weather) to a scenic overlook of Hells Canyon at Hat Point. But our route lead south along the Imnaha River, and from there it was strictly rutted dirt roads to the trailhead. Ken is a stockily-built character in his early 40s, with a wry grin and enormous energy. He needs every bit of his strength and energy when it comes to packing up all the gear for a party of eight riders and loading it on the backs of his long-suffering mules. But that morning he accomplished the task in record time and we were on the trail before it began to get hot. By the time we dismounted for lunch on top of Freezeout Saddle, however, we were hoping for a

Above: *Mining has played a part in the boom-and-bust economy of the Wallowa Country since white settlers first arrived. Theses ruins of an old smelter at Eureka Bar in Hells Canyon are reminders of the region's intriguing history.*
Left: *The Snake River winds through Hells Canyon, the deepest gorge in North America.* DAVID JENSEN PHOTOS

Above: The Lakes Basin attracts most visitors to Oregon's largest designated wilderness area, the Eagle Cap Wilderness in the Wallowa Mountains. © GARY BRAASCH

Right: Outfitters guide their guests on horseback through the challenging terrain of the Hells Canyon National Recreation Area. CHARLIE BORLAND

Facing page: The Matterhorn is the highest of several granitic peaks in the Eagle Cap Wilderness that soar to almost 10,000'. DAVID JENSEN

little of the freezing weather that the name implied. Even though it was only the first week in May, the temperature in Hells Canyon was well over 100°F—and rising! Even the sweeping views of mountain peaks all around us couldn't take our minds off that heat. In every season, Hells Canyon is a place of tremendous extremes—hot and cold, wet and dry—sometimes all in the same day!

That afternoon we followed Saddle Creek down the length of its canyon and camped at an old, abandoned homestead along the Snake River. We had reached the bottom of America's deepest gorge and as evening fell, the light faded slowly. As we watched the colors change on the canyon walls, Ken's helper, Dave Piland, spied a group

of bighorn sheep as they grazed the steep terrain of the canyon wall across the river. Later, around the campfire, Ken pulled out a book of cowboy poetry and kept us all in stitches with his highly dramatic reading.

The next day Ken and Dave were up and packed before the sun rose over the canyon wall. Our horses followed the trail along the Snake River, up and over the Devil's Staircase, a narrow, rocky passage where a mistake by horse or rider could mean a nasty fall to the river, 200' below. Along the rocky walls grew cacti with delicate pink blossoms, a fitting symbol of this rugged canyon of contrasts. Our days in Hells Canyon were long and hot, but the experience was unforgettable—I'd return in a minute.

I've also ridden with one of Ken Wick's pack strings into the Eagle Cap Wilderness, high in the Wallowa Mountains. Although it's only 50 miles or so from where we began our Hells Canyon adventure, the Eagle Cap feels like another planet. This is Oregon's largest official Wilderness Area, encompassing over 300,000 acres, with snow-capped mountains that soar to almost 10,000' in altitude. It's an area that shares its geologic heritage with the Rocky Mountains and, unlike the symmetrical volcanic peaks in western Oregon's Cascade Range, these mountains are sprinkled with colorful granitic out-croppings that drop steeply into heavily glaciated hanging valleys.

Our trail began in a dense stand of fir trees at the head of Wallowa Lake. The pack string wound up the side of a U-shaped valley, scrubbed by glaciers in some distant ice age, and emerged at Aneroid Lake, where we stopped for lunch. Once you've cleared the tree line in the Eagle Cap Wilderness, the vistas seem to stretch off into the haze in every direction. Riding on horseback across this terrain, your head feels like it's on a swivel, as you try to take in all the sights.

We camped that night at the head of the basin of the North Fork of the Imnaha River. The whole world seemed to be spread out at our feet. Over the ridgeline to the west was the Lakes Basin, where dozens of pristine lakes draw most of the visitors to this big wilderness. But Ken was determined to avoid "crowds of people," as he put it, and over the next few days he led us down canyons and over basins that are rarely visited by human beings. Traveling with horses and mules made it all possible—the horses enabled us to cover many miles, and without the mules we would have been limited only to the gear we could carry on our backs.

Instead, we dined on Ken's Western-style barbecued steaks and other delights around the campfire. At night we gazed at a sky filled to the brim with stars. We saw deer and elk, trout and salmon, soaring hawks and chirping pikas. Even though it was early August, we awoke one morning to frozen water bottles and snow-covered tents. In short, it was a delightful mountain adventure—the kind everyone should experience at least once. But once wasn't enough for me. I returned to see the Eagle Cap from another perspective—this time leading a string of llamas to carry our loads. Stanlynn Daugherty operates an outfitting business called Hurricane Creek Llamas, using llamas as the pack animals for hiking trips into the Eagle Cap Wilderness. She raises her llama herd, which ranges in size

Above: Natives of the South American Andes, llamas now are used to carry gear for hikers on the steep alpine trails in the Wallowa Mountains. J.A. LOSI

Right: Dry, powdery snow provides the perfect conditions for a winter back-country tour in the Eagle Cap Wilderness. DAVID JENSEN

from 15 to 30 animals, on a small ranch outside the town of Joseph. Her place has even become a sort of tourist attraction, as carloads of visitors cruise slowly by each summer, eyeing the strange-looking critters that graze peacefully in the pasture by the house.

Natives of the South American Andes, llamas have long been used as pack animals in alpine country and willingly carry 50 to 100 pounds of gear, depending on the animal's size and age. That means tremendous freedom for hikers, who carry only a day pack with rain gear, a sweater and lunch. Stanlynn assigns each hiker his or her own llama, to lead on a short rope as the group makes its way up the trail. The lamas sport descriptive names, such as Strider, Cupcake or Partner, and each llama is identifiable by the unique color pattern of its wool, as well as its extremely expressive long ears and large eyes. As the trip progressed, we all found ourselves fascinated by the distinctive personalities of our personal "beasts of burden."

Our hike led us up Hurricane Creek into the Eagle Cap Wilderness. We climbed a steep trail—with our llamas puffing and panting in our ears—to a glacial bowl at the base of 9,800′ Sacajawea Peak. Here we camped and explored the rocky basin to our heart's content. In the evening, we devoured Stanlynn's gourmet cooking and watched the full moon rise over the basin rim as swapped stories around the campfire. Even though it was Labor Day weekend and the weather was perfect, we didn't encounter a single other party of hikers during our stay.

Even though wilderness treks are a great way to see this part of the state, there are plenty of other things to do in the Wallowa Valley. Most visitors are attracted to Wallowa Lake, where one of the state's biggest and busiest state parks offers a convenient base for camping and exploration. You can ride a cable tramway to the top of nearby Mount Howard—at 8,200′—for fantastic views of the mountains and valleys all around. On top, there are hiking trails and even a deli, where you can eat your lunch outside and enjoy the view.

Back down at the south end of the lake, try a meal or an overnight stay at the newly refurbished Wallowa Lake Lodge. Or sample several other eating spots and vacation lodges at this bustling little summer resort area. The lake itself offers good fishing, waterskiing, sailing and windsurfing. Wallowa Lake is four miles long, glacial in origin, quite deep, and remains very cold throughout the year.

Just beyond the north end of Wallowa Lake, on the outskirts of the town of Joseph, is a bed and breakfast inn

called the Bed, Bread and Trail. It's run by Ethel and Jim Chandler, who left their secure careers in Portland a few years ago to establish a guest house in the Wallowa Valley. Jim has done a remarkable job of remodeling their home into a hostelry and Ethel's hand is obvious in the comfortable furnishings that highlight the airy upstairs rooms they rent to guests. Together, they also serve up a sumptuous breakfast meal.

Just a few blocks north is the Wallowa County Museum, where an excellent display of artifacts collected from both the Nez Perce tribe and the early white settlers

in this area can be seen. Nez Perce influence in this valley is still quite tangible, not only in the names of places and businesses, but in the attitudes of the local residents. Like the Nez Perce before them, today's Wallowa County citizens are independent and proud of their valley homeland. And they are a little reluctant to show off the scenic splendor of their valley to visitors, for fear they might be overrun by a new wave of homesteaders. However, Wallowa County residents also can't resist a good party, so each year they invite visitors to come share their festivals. In July, a rodeo and parade highlight Chief Joseph Days in

Above: *Hurricane Creek is one of the many clear, cold streams that drain the Wallowa Mountains in northeastern Oregon.*
Left: *Many summer visitors to the Eagle Cap Wilderness find solitude by carrying all their gear on their backs.* DAVID JENSEN PHOTOS

Above: *The town of Joseph sits at the foot of Wallowa Lake, in the shadow of the Wallowa Mountains.*
Top right: *Wallowa County residents still are a bit reluctant to show off their mountain valley, for fear they might be overrun by a new wave of homesteaders.*
Bottom right: *Northeastern Oregon is cowboy country and rodeos play an important part in annual festivities.* DAVID JENSEN PHOTOS

the town of Joseph. In mid-September, Enterprise puts on Hells Canyon Mule Days, and later that same month, a three-day Alpenfest is held at Wallowa Lake.

Enterprise is the center of commercial services in Wallowa County and the logical place to restock food and gasoline, or to secure a motel room for the night. While you're in Enterprise, take a few minutes to walk through the downtown section and look at the many refurbished buildings constructed from native stone. The Wallowa

County Courthouse occupies an entire block in the center of town and is a fine example of the region's pioneer architecture. Across the street, the Bookloft bookstore nestles in another historic building and offers a surprising collection of new and used books, as well as a fine art gallery in the rear. My favorite restaurant in Enterprise is called A Country Place on Pete's Pond—and that pretty well describes the ambience. Located on an old log mill pond, the restaurant features hearty home-style cooking and freshly baked breads and rolls. If the weather is right, it's a treat to sit outside on the deck and toss bread crumbs to the ducks, geese and trout who call the pond home.

Perhaps the most unique destination resort in Wallowa County is simply called The Horse Ranch. It's the only private resort in Oregon that's actually located inside a designated wilderness area—on the banks of the Minam River in the Eagle Cap Wilderness. The only way to get to The Horse Ranch is over a trail—either by hiking or on horseback—or by airplane. Owner Cal Henry was kind enough to fly me to the ranch in his private plane on one of his regular morning flights from the Enterprise airport. The high-altitude views of the countryside were magnificent, but the thrill of swooping down the Minam River canyon and landing on the rugged airstrip next to his lodge was more than enough to take your breath away. The eight cabins at The Horse Ranch are a rustic home base for hunting and fishing trips into the surrounding wilderness. Each guest is furnished with a horse for basic transportation, and overnight pack trips can be organized from the ranch.

Unless you're heading north toward the Washington border, you'll probably leave Wallowa County the way you arrived, on State Route 82. If you happen to visit during ski season, Spout Springs Ski Area is just a few miles northwest of Elgin on State Route 204. The other downhill ski area in the region, Anthony Lakes, is reached by exiting I-84 at the little town of North Powder, north of Baker, and following signs west to the ski area. If you're headed west on I-84, plan to stop at Immigrant Springs State Park near Meacham, in the Blue Mountains. This oasis was the resting spot for pioneer wagon trains after they had completed the long pull up the mountain grade. Here the weary immigrants prepared for the treacherous descent to the Columbia Plateau. Meacham also has another distinction: it's the area where Oregon's coldest annual temperatures are recorded almost every winter.

Above: *Cabins at The Horse Ranch, Oregon's only private resort inside a designated wilderness area, perch on the banks of the Minam River.*
MARK HOY

Left: *A logging truck winds its way up the Minam Grade in northeastern Oregon's canyon country.*
DAN DAVIDSON

Columbia Gorge Country

Columbia River National Recreation Area

Hood River

The Old Columbia Gorge Highway

Above: *Purple-eyed grass in the Columbia Gorge.*
Right: *The Columbia River Gorge, one of the truly distinctive terrains in the West.* PHOTOS © GARY BRAASCH

The Columbia Gorge on Oregon's northern border is a multifaceted scenic wonder that no visitor to the state should miss. Unfortunately, many do miss it—especially the drivers who zip through on Interstate 84 and later tell their friends, "Gee, what a great drive that is through the Columbia Gorge!"

The gorge is like a beautifully decorated layer cake that's made up of different flavors. It looks delicious on the surface, but the real satisfaction comes once you probe beneath the visual frosting and discover all the intriguing secrets inside. Rubbernecking your way through the gorge at 65 mph may be a thrill for someone who's never seen it. But once you begin to understand that you're passing through one of the truly distinctive pieces of terrain in the West, you'll certainly want to slow down and explore.

In 1986, Congress acknowledged the special attributes of the Columbia Gorge by designating it a National Scenic Area. Conservationists long had sought some sort of protection for the natural wonders, which have withstood human use and abuse for thousands of years.

One of the first impressions you get as you drive through the gorge is the concentration of commerce and human traffic along the river. Power lines drape the hillsides, huge grain barges lumber downriver, and trailer trucks flow steadily along the interstate, all part of the Columbia's role as the great working river of the West.

There's also great natural beauty in the Columbia Gorge. And the farther you get from the river, the more you can hear the wind whistling through the canyons and see the shape of time and water at work on the land. Steep rock walls loom over the landscape. Waterfalls leap off the escarpments and flutter down to earth in misty rainbows. In springtime, wildflowers compete with apple and pear blossoms to dazzle the eye. You could spend a lifetime exploring the Columbia Gorge and still experience something new with each new season. The present topography of the gorge is the result of millions of years of interaction between intermittent lava flows and the constant, eroding work of water. The Columbia River drains an area almost as large as Texas, far north into British Columbia and east into Montana and Wyoming. Much of this area was covered by a succession of huge lava flows millions of years ago. The lava often flowed down the ancestral

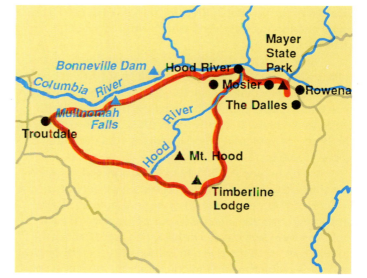

The eastern end of the Columbia Gorge opens up into rolling hillsides, revealing the complex geology beneath. DAVID JENSEN

In the western end of the Columbia Gorge, such as at Oneonta Gorge, visitors can explore the "greatest concentration of high waterfalls in North America." © GARY BRAASCH

channel of the Columbia River to the sea, each time hardening and forcing the river farther north as it re-cut its channel.

More recently, the Cascade volcanoes emerged and built a wall of mountains, through which the Columbia River eventually cut to reach the ocean. But the events which most profoundly influenced the formation of the gorge as we know it were a series of gigantic floods, called the Bretz (or Spokane) Floods, which swept through the gorge 15,000 to 12,800 years ago.

Ice dams, some 2,000' high, had formed during the previous ice age and impounded lakes, which contained a volume of water equal to half of present Lake Michigan and spread over the area that is now Montana. When the ice dams were breached, a volume of water 10 times the current flow of all the rivers in the world rushed through eastern Washington and Oregon, scouring the landscape.

In the gorge, all the soils and every living thing below 1,000' in elevation were scraped away in many places. Giant boulders of granite, coated with ice, were swept along by the flow and eventually deposited high in tributary streams, where they can be seen today. On many of the steep precipices in the gorge, soil and vegetation still have not reestablished themselves, thousands of years later.

In recent times, landslides have had the most dramatic effect on the appearance of the gorge and the course of the Columbia River. Near the present site of Cascade Locks, an earthquake several hundred years ago probably was the trigger for a landslide that completely dammed the Columbia. Until the river was able to erode the rocks and soil that blocked it, the native people who fished along the river could walk across a land bridge to the opposite shore. They celebrated this event with the legend of the "Bridge of the Gods." Today, a steel bridge with the same name spans the river nearby.

When the Columbia finally eroded away the Bridge of the Gods, the remaining boulders formed a treacherous new rapid, known to the white settlers who tried to run it in their river boats as the Cascades of the Columbia. There is some evidence to suggest that the entire mountain range which the Columbia cuts through in this area, the Cascade Range, took its name from these rapids. Today, the Cascades of the Columbia are buried under the deep, still pool behind Bonneville Dam.

The Columbia River is the largest river in North America that empties into the Pacific Ocean. Because its river valley provides the only ready access to the ocean from the continental interior of the Northwest, the Columbia Gorge served as the passageway for most European settlers who explored the region. Many brave men and women ended their journey on the famous Oregon Trail by floating their possessions through the gorge, perhaps the most dangerous leg of the long journey.

Glimpses of the hardship endured by pioneer settlers, as well as an array of scenic wonders, can be seen by driving the old Columbia River Scenic Highway. Although the new interstate highway was built along the same roadbed as the old scenic highway in many places, two sections of the old highway remain, and are well worth exploring.

Completed in 1915, the Scenic Highway was considered one of the engineering marvels of its time. It was the first paved highway in Oregon and the first automobile road to connect the western valleys with the eastern plateaus of the state. It twists and turns along steep hillsides, forcing drivers to slow down and enabling passengers to enjoy the majestic views of the gorge. Be sure to stop and look closely at some of the detailed and carefully crafted bridges along the way.

You can gain access to a 24-mile section of the old Scenic Highway from the west by exiting I-84 at Troutdale or at the Sandy River. Follow signs for the Scenic Highway (U.S. Route 30). Do stop at Crown Point, where Vista House Visitor Center offers a sweeping view of the western end of the gorge. Pick up the brochure "Touring the Columbia Gorge" for a list of stops along the old highway.

Beyond Vista House, the roadside holds what Oregon's most eminent living geologist, John Eliot Allen,

Above: Historic Vista House at Crown Point commands a panoramic view of the western end of the Columbia Gorge.
Left: Many bridges along the Old Scenic Highway reveal an attention to detail and craftsmanship no longer associated with highway construction. PHOTOS © GARY BRAASCH

Above: Bonneville Dam was the first of the large mainstem dams to harness the power of the Columbia River. © GARY BRAASCH
Right: Wildflowers bloom in profusion in the Mt. Hood Wilderness Area. CHARLIE BORLAND

Facing page, left: Multnomah Falls, actually a double falls with a total drop of 620', attracts travelers to its visitor center and beautiful old stone lodge building. © GARY BRAASCH
Right: Horsetail Falls shows off its fall colors. CHARLIE BORLAND

calls "the greatest concentration of high waterfalls in North America." There are 11 waterfalls more 100' high that can be seen from the road. The most popular is Multnomah Falls, which is really a double falls with a total drop of 620'. There's a visitor center here and a beautiful old stone lodge, built in 1925. A paved path leads all the way to the top of Multnomah Falls, a climb that's guaranteed to make most hikers stop for a few deep breaths along the way, but worth every step for the panoramic views.

If you decide to avoid the crowds at Multnomah Falls, there are many other waterfalls to visit. Some are along the highway, others require a little hiking to reach. One of my favorites is Oneonta Falls, where you'll hike a quarter mile right in the creekbed through a narrow gorge to reach the falls. But there are so many interesting sights and trails to explore along this section of the Scenic Highway, the best advice is to get a good map, or the Forest Service brochure "Forest Trails of the Columbia Gorge."

At Ainsworth State Park, the Scenic Highway ends and you'll have to continue on Interstate 84. However, there are some attractive rest areas and state parks scattered along I-84 as you pass through the gorge, each one offering unique views of the river canyon and possibilities for hikes or camping. The visitor center at Bonneville Dam also is worth a stop. Here you can see displays that tell the story of how the Columbia River's power has been harnessed by a series of dams. There are also viewing areas where big salmon and steelhead pass as they make their way through the fish ladders and around the dam.

The eastern section of the old Scenic Highway begins at the little town of Mosier (take exit 69 off I-84) and climbs along a plateau above the river and the freeway for nine miles to The Dalles. You're now in the more open, arid end of the gorge, where views up and down the river extend for many miles, without the west side's big fir trees to obstruct your view.

For geology buffs, the eastern end of the Gorge provides easy viewing of the layers from various lava flows along the canyon walls. The long series of flows that slant down to the water on the Washington side of the river are collectively called the Mosier Syncline.

There's one stop along this eastern section of the Scenic Highway that shouldn't be missed. At the sign indicating the parking area for Mayer State Park, pull into a circular overlook area. In addition to the wonderful vistas up and down the gorge here, you're now in the middle of the Tom McCall Rowena Preserve. This 200-acre tract of relatively undisturbed land was purchased from private owners by The Nature Conservancy, a conservation group that specializes in acquiring and managing areas of critical environmental concern.

Named in part for a former Oregon governor who was nationally known for his progressive environmental ideas, the Tom McCall Rowena Preserve is home in spring

to some of the showiest wildflower displays seen anywhere in the gorge. Many of the plants here grow only in the gorge, so keep a sharp eye out for unusual-looking flowers as you hike the meandering trails. The preserve land was one of the areas swept clean by the Bretz floods, but the wild grasses and wildflowers have reseeded themselves in shallow new soil, primarily composed of weathered volcanic ash from periodic eruptions of nearby Mount St. Helens.

Beyond the Tom McCall Rowena Preserve, the Scenic Highway descends off the plateau in a snaking set of switchbacks called the Rowena Loops. After you finish the scenic loop, I'd recommend returning west to the town of Hood River, an excellent central base of operations for further explorations of the gorge.

Hood River grew up as a processing and shipping center for the bounteous apple and pear harvests nearby, but has recently gone through an intriguing metamorphosis. A few years ago, the town was on the economic critical list, after its big fruit-processing operations closed. However, a few adventurous young athletes discovered that the stiff summer winds howling through this part of the gorge created some of the finest, most consistent, windsurfing conditions in North America.

This rapidly growing sport, combining sailing and surfing, caught on. Suddenly, the sleepy little town of Hood River was playing host each summer to a growing crowd of young, affluent, fun-loving board sailors. As might be expected, there were some cultural clashes between the town's old guard and the brash newcomers. But these days, most long-time Hood River residents have come to see windsurfing as their economic salvation, and many of the windsurfers have discovered that Hood River is a wonderful place to settle down, raise families, and begin new businesses. The windsurfers have become a significant part of the economic and social fabric of Hood River.

For a close-up look at windsurfing, take Exit 64 off I-84 on the east side of Hood River. There's a visitor information center here where you can pick up tips on lodging and dining in the area. The Hood River County Historical Museum is also nearby (open during the summer months) and offers a glimpse of the area's colorful, rollicking past as a river port.

But the big attraction is the Sailpark and Marina, where windsurfers gather during the summer months to check wind conditions, converse about their sport in a dialect of English that's totally foreign to outsiders, and launch their sail-and-surfboard combinations out into the tricky currents of the Columbia River. On windy days, scores of brightly colored sailboards crisscross the river, providing dazzling viewing for spectators at this riverside perch.

One of the indications of Hood River's new prosperity is the number of post-Victorian homes that have been refurbished on the town's hillsides. Several of the old homes have been transformed into bed and breakfast operations, to accommodate the crush of windsurfers who arrive here for summer tournaments and other gatherings. The old Columbia Gorge Hotel, originally built in 1921 by timber baron Simon Benson to encourage tourist travel along the Columbia, has been restored as a country inn with 46 guest rooms. A lavish farm breakfast is included in the room price. Befitting a gorge institution, the hotel even has its own private waterfall out back. You'll find the

Above: *The Rowena Loops, part of the Old Columbia Gorge Scenic Highway, west of The Dalles.* © GARY BRAASCH **Top:** *Orchards in the Hood River Valley and wildflowers dazzle the eyes with blossoms.* DON MEGRATH **Left:** *Windsurfing boosts communities such as Hood River.* JOHN DAUGIRDA **Facing page:** *The Columbia Gorge is best experienced by driving secondary roads and hiking the forest trails.* © GARY BRAASCH

Columbia Gorge Hotel near exit 62 off I-84. Next to the hotel is a tasting room for Hood River Vineyards and across the freeway a new winery called Three Rivers has a tasting room in a lovely turn-of-the-century home. Just up the hill is a turnoff for the Stonehenge Inn, a delightful old country house where elegant evening meals are served. Call ahead for reservations.

In downtown Hood River, in a section of old, abandoned cannery buildings, a group of young people are working on an ambitious undertaking. They've established the Hood River Brewing Company, hoping to catch the wave of new brew-pubs that have become popular in metropolitan areas across the country. They serve their Full Sail Golden Ale (featuring a bright windsurfing sail on the label) in their shiny new pub quarters, where you can either watch the colorful windsurfers below on the Columbia River or gaze through big plate-glass windows at the brewery workers as they produce their new Oregon beer.

Be sure to take a stroll around Hood River's bustling downtown area, where new restaurants, boutiques and, especially, windsurfing equipment stores are springing up at a dizzying rate.

Or try a drive up the Hood River Valley, where you can glimpse striking views of snow-capped Mt. Hood to the south. It's an especially scenic drive in spring, when the apple and pear blossoms are in bloom on the acres of orchards that grace the valley. Maps and a description of a scenic loop drive are at the visitor information center.

State Route 35 is the main road south through the Hood River Valley and the return loop takes you along Hood River on Route 281. You can also make a much longer loop by continuing south on Route 35 around the base of Mt. Hood, until the road intersects with U.S. Highway 26, which will return you west to Portland.

If you make the longer loop, don't miss the famous Timberline Lodge, reached by an access road off U.S. 26. Built as a Depression-era project in 1937, Timberline Lodge is a masterpiece—an example of what skilled craftspeople can create with native stone, wood, iron, fiber and their own imaginations. Like many of the other sights in or near the Columbia Gorge, Timberline Lodge is a rare gem that requires only time and attention to reveal its natural luster.

Above: *Mt. Hood, Oregon's highest peak, dominates the skyline above the Columbia Gorge.* CHARLIE BORLAND
Facing page: *The Hood River Sailpark and Marina during a rare calm moment.* © GARY BRAASCH

References
and
Addresses

General

Alt, David D., and Donald W. Hyndman, *Roadside Geology of Oregon,* Mountain Press Publishing Co., Missoula, MT, 1978.

Insight Guide: The Pacific Northwest ($15.95), published by APA Productions, Ltd., distributed by Graphic Arts Center Publishing, P.O. Box 10306, Portland, OR 97210. (503) 226-2402.

Oakley, Myrna, *Bed and Breakfast Northwest,* Chronicle Books, San Francisco, CA, 1984.

The Official Oregon State Travel Guide ($3.00) & *Oregon Traveler's Guide to Accommodations,* Economic Development Department, Tourism Division, 595 Cottage St. N.E., Salem, OR 97310.

Official Highway Map of Oregon, Oregon Department of Transportation, State Highway Division, Salem, OR 97310.

Oregon Guides & Packers Directory, P.O. Box 3797, Portland, OR, 97208. 503-234-3268. Central listing of river guides, back-country packers and other outfitters in Oregon.

Oregon State Parks, 525 Trade Street S.E., Salem, OR 97310. Ask for the *Guide to State Parks* and the *Oregon Bicycling Guide,* as well as information on specific state parks.

Rogue River

Arman, Florence, with Glen Wooldridge, *The Rogue: A River to Run,* Wildwood Press, 209 SW Wildwood Ave., Grants Pass, OR 97526, 1982.

Grey, Zane, *Tales of Freshwater Fishing,* Harper and Brothers, New York, NY, 1928.

Northwest Whitewater Excursions, P.O. Box 10754, Eugene, OR 97440. (503) 342-1222.

Orange Torpedo Trips, Inc., P.O. Box 1111, Grants Pass, OR 97526. (503) 479-5061.

Oregon Caves Chateau, Oregon Caves, OR 97523. (503) Oregon Caves Toll Station No. 1.

Purdom, William B., *Guide to the Geology and Lore of the Wild Reach of the Rogue River, Oregon,* Museum of Natural History, Bulletin No. 22, University of Oregon, Eugene, Oregon 97403, 1977.

Quinn, James M., James W. Quinn, and James G. King, *Professional Guides' Handbook to the Rogue River Canyon,* Educational Adventures, Inc., 2941 Doctors Park Dr., Medford, OR 97501, 1979.

Rand Visitor Center (river permits and information), 14335 Galice Road, Merlin, OR 97532. (503) 479-3735.

Rogue River Reservations (lodge and jet boat information), P.O. Box 548, Gold Beach, OR 97444. (503) 247-6504 or 247-6022.

Rogue Wilderness, Inc. (lodge information and reservations), Box 1647, Grants Pass, OR 97526. (503) 479-9554.

Siskiyou Vineyards, 6220 Caves Hwy., Cave Junction, OR 97523. (503) 592-3727.

Bandon

Bandon Chamber of Commerce (information on lodging, restaurants and attractions), P.O. Box 1515, Bandon, OR 97411. (503) 347-9616.

Brown, Vinson, *Exploring Pacific Coast Tide Pools,* Naturegraph Company, Healdsburg, CA, 1966.

Oregon Dunes National Recreation Area, Siuslaw National Forest, 855 Highway Ave., Reedsport, OR 97467. (503) 271-3611.

South Slough National Estuarine Reserve, P.O. Box 5417, Charleston, OR 97420. (503) 888-5558.

Spindrift Bed & Breakfast, 2990 Beach Loop Rd., Bandon, OR 97411. (503) 347-2275.

Astoria

Columbia River Maritime Museum, 1792 Marine Drive, Astoria, OR 97103. (503) 325-2323. Admission: Adults—$2.50, students and senior citizens—$1.50.

Flavel House, Clatsop County Historical Society, 1618 Exchange, Astoria, OR 97103. (503) 325-2563. Admission: Adults—$2.00, children—$0.75.

Fort Clatsop National Memorial, Rt. 3, Box 6045-FC, Astoria, OR 97103. (503) 861-2471. Admission: $1.00 per adult.

Gault, Vera Whitney, *Walking Tour of Astoria, Oregon,* 1393 Franklin Ave., Astoria, OR 97103, 1985.

Greater Astoria Area Chamber of Commerce & Visitor Center (information on lodging, restaurants and attractions), 111 W. Marine Drive, Astoria, OR 97103. (503) 325-6311.

North Coast Bed and Breakfast Association (pamphlet listing area bed and breakfasts), P.O. Box 383, Astoria, OR 97103.

Rosebriar Inn, 636 Fourteenth Street, Astoria, OR 97103.

Tillamook Cheese, P.O. Box 313, Tillamook, OR 97141.

Wineries

Alpine Vineyards, 25904 Green Peak Road, Alpine OR 97456. (503) 424-5851.

Chateau Benoit Winery, 6580 N.E. Mineral Springs Rd., Carlton, OR 97111. (503) 864-2991.

Discover Oregon Wineries, Oregon Winegrowers Association, P.O. Box 6590, Portland, OR 97228-6590. (503) 233-2377.

The Eyrie Vineyards, 935 East 10th St., McMinnville, OR 97128. (503) 472-6315.

Forgeron Vineyard, 89697 Sheffler Road, Elmira, OR 97437. (503) 935-1117.

Hinman Vineyards, 27012 Briggs Hill Rd., Eugene, OR 97405. (503) 345-1945.

Knudsen Erath Winery, 17000 N.E. Knudsen Lane, Dundee OR 97115. (503) 538-3318.

Sokol Blosser Winery, P.O. Box 199, Sokol Blosser Lane, Dundee, OR 97115. (503) 864-2282.

Cascade

Blue River Ranger Station (U.S. Forest Service), Blue River, OR 97413. (503) 822-3317.

Breitenbush Retreat Center, P.O. Box 578, Detroit, OR 97342. (503) 854-3501.

Detroit Ranger Station (U.S. Forest Service), Star Route, Box 320, Mill City, OR 97360. (503) 854-3366.

McKenzie Ranger Station (U.S. Forest Service), McKenzie Bridge, OR 97413. (503) 822-3381.

Oakridge Ranger Station (U.S. Forest Service), 46375 Highway 58, Westfir, OR 97492. (503) 782-2291.

Oregon State Highway Patrol (recorded information on winter road conditions), (503) 238-8400.

Willamette National Forest, Eugene Federal Building, P.O. Box 10607, Eugene, OR 97401. (503) 687-6521. Forest maps and recreation information available. Ask for maps for Mt. Jefferson, French Pete and Three Sisters Wilderness Areas, as well as the following publications: *McKenzie River National Recreation Trail, McKenzie Pass: A Part of Oregon's Volcanic Wonderland, Willamette Pass Ski Tours,* and *The Waldo Lake Area.*

North Umpqua

Garden Valley Winery, 251 Camino Francisco, Roseburg, OR 97470. (503) 673-3010.

Girardet Wine Cellars, 895 Reston Road, Roseburg, OR 97470. (503) 679-7252.

Henry Estate Winery, P.O. Box 26, Hwy. 9, Umpqua, OR 97486. (503) 459-5120.

Hillcrest Vineyards, 240 Vineyard Lane, Roseburg, OR 97470. (503) 673-3709.

Jonicole Vineyards, 491 Winery Lane, Roseburg, OR 97470. (503) 679-5771.

North Umpqua Ranger District, Umpqua National Forest, Glide, OR 97443. (503) 496-3532. Maps and recreation information available.

Ouzel Outfitters, P.O. Box 11217, Eugene, OR 97440. (503) 747-2236.

The Steamboat Inn, Box 36, Toketee Route, Idleyld Park, OR 97447. (503) 498-2411.

Wildlife Safari, P.O. Box 1600, Winston, OR 97496-0231. (503) 679-6761. Admission charged.

Klamath Basin

Klamath Basin National Wildlife Refuges, Route 1, Box 74, Tulelake, CA 96134. (916) 667-2231.

Lava Beds National Monument, Box 867, Tulelake, CA 96134.

Take It Easy Fly Fishing Resort, P.O. Box 408, Fort Klamath, OR 97626. (503) 381-2328.

Bend

Bend Chamber of Commerce, 164 N.W. Hawthorne Ave., Bend, OR 97701. (503) 382-3221. Information on dining, lodging and points of interest in the Bend area.

Bend Research, Inc., 64550 Research Road, Bend, OR 97701-8599. (503) 382-2713.

Crane Prairie Resort, P.O. Box 1171, Bend, OR 97709. Summer phone: (503) 385-2173. Winter phone: (503) 382-2787.

Deschutes National Forest, 1645 East Highway 20, Bend, OR 97701. (503) 388-2715. Maps and recreational information available, including *The Lava Butte Geological Area* pamphlet.

Elk Lake Resort, P.O. Box 789, Bend, OR 97709. (503) Mobile phone YP7-3954.

The High Desert Museum, 59800 S. Highway 97, Bend, OR 97702. (503) 382-4754.

Mt. Bachelor Ski and Summer Resort, P.O. Box 1031, Bend, OR 97709-1031. (800) 547-6858 (outside Oregon), (503) 382-8334 (in Oregon).

Rock Springs Guest Ranch, 64201 Tyler Road, Bend, OR 97701. (503) 382-1957.

Sunriver Lodge and Resort, Sunriver, OR 97707. (503) 593-1221.

John Day

John Day Fossil Beds National Monument, 420 W. Main, John Day, OR 97845. (503) 575-0721.

Ochoco National Forest, P.O. Box 490, Prineville, OR 97754. (503) 447-6247. Maps, campground and recreation information.

Malheur

Bureau of Land Management, Burns District, 74 S. Alvord St., Burns, OR 97720. (503) 573-2071. Maps, campground and recreation information. Ask for *Diamond Craters: Oregon's Geologic Gem* brochure.

Bureau of Land Management, Vale District, 365 A St., P.O. Box 700, Vale, OR 97918. (503) 473-3144. Maps and recreation information on Owyhee River area.

Desert Trail Association, P.O. Box 589, Burns, OR 97720.

Frenchglen Hotel State Wayside, Frenchglen, OR 97736. (503) 493-2825.

Malheur Field Station, P.O. Box 260-E, Princeton, OR 97721. (503) 493-2629.

Malheur National Wildlife Refuge, P.O. Box 113, Burns, OR 97720. (503) 493-2323.

Wallowa Country

Anthony Lakes Ski Area, P.O. Box 3040, La Grande, OR 97850. (503) 856-3277.

The Bed, Bread & Trail Inn (Ethel and Jim Chandler, innkeepers), 700 S. Main, Joseph, OR 97846. (503) 432-9765.

The Bookloft, 107 East Main Street, Enterprise, OR 97828. (503) 426-3351.

Eagle Cap Ranger District, Wallowa-Whitman National Forest, Enterprise, OR 97828. (503) 426-3104. Maps and recreation information on Eagle Cap Wilderness Area, as well as surrounding forest areas.

Hells Canyon National Recreation Area, P.O. Box 490, Enterprise, OR 97828. (503) 426-3151. Maps and recreation information on Hells Canyon area.

The Horse Ranch, c/o High Country Outfitters, P.O. Box 26, Joseph, OR 97846. (503) 432-9171.

Hurricane Creek Llamas (Stanlynn Daugherty), Route 1, Box 123, Enterprise, OR 97828. (503) 432-4455.

Outback Ranch Outfitters (Ken Wick), P.O. Box 384, Joseph, OR 97846. (503) 432-1721.

Spout Springs Ski Area, Route 1, Weston, OR 97886. (503) 566-2015.

Wallowa County Chamber of Commerce, P.O. Box 427, Enterprise, OR 97828. (503) 426-4622. Information on lodging, dining and activities in Wallowa County.

Wallowa County Museum, S. Main Street, Joseph, OR 97846.

Columbia Gorge

Allen, John Eliot, *The Magnificent Gateway: A Layman's Guide to the Geology of the Columbia River Gorge,* Timber Press, P.O. Box 1631, Beaverton, OR 97075, 1984.

Columbia Gorge Country Inns and Wineries (brochure), Columbia Gorge Country Inns and Wineries Assoc., P.O. Box 797, Bingen, WA 98605.

Right: In the Wallowa Mountains.
DAVID JENSEN

Columbia Gorge District, Mt. Hood National Forest, 31520 S.E. Woodward Road, Troutdale, OR 97060. (503) 695-2276. Maps, camping and recreation information. Ask for *Forest Trails of the Columbia Gorge* map.

Columbia Gorge Hotel, 4000 West Cliff Drive, Hood River, OR 97031. (503) 386-5566.

Hood River Brewing Company, 506 Columbia Street, Hood River, OR 97031. (503) 386-2281.

Hood River County Historical Museum, Port Marina Park, Hood River, OR 97031.

Hood River Vineyard, 4693 Westwood Drive, Hood River, OR 97031. (503) 386-3772.

Hood River Visitors Council, Port Marina Park, Hood River, OR 97031. (503) 386-2000. Lodging, dining and activities information for Hood River area.

Three Rivers Winery, 275 Country Club Road, Hood River, OR 97031. (503) 386-5453.

Timberline Lodge, Government Camp, OR 97028. (503) 231-5400.

Touring the Columbia Gorge (pamphlet), Columbia River Gorge Marketing, P.O. Box 118, Hood River, OR 97031. (800) 222-8660 outside Oregon, (503) 386-6262 inside Oregon.

AMERICAN GEOGRAPHIC PUBLISHING

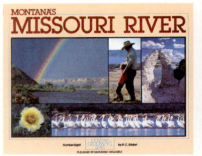

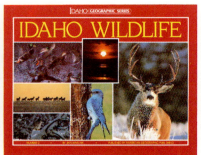

EACH BOOK HAS ABOUT 100 PAGES, 11" X 8½", 120 TO 170 COLOR PHOTO-GRAPHS

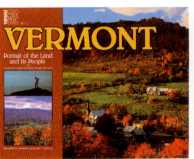

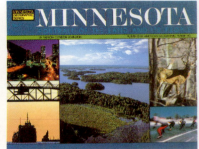

Enjoy, See, Understand America State by State

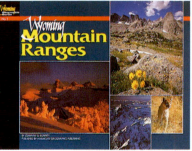

American Geographic Publishing
Geographic Series of the States

Lively, colorful, beautifully illustrated books specially written for these series explain land form, animals and plants, economy, lifestyle and history of each state or feature. Generous color photography brings each state to life and makes each book a treat to turn to frequently. The geographic series format is designed to give you more information than coffee-table photo books, yet so much more color photography than simple guide books.

Each book includes:

• Colorful maps
• Valuable descriptions and charts of features such as volcanoes and glaciers
• Up-to-date understanding of environmental problems where man and nature are in conflict
• References for additional reading, agencies and offices to contact for more information
• Special sections portraying people in their homes, at work, in the countryside

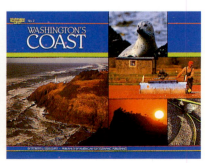

for more information write:
American Geographic Publishing
P.O. Box 5630
Helena, Montana 59604